Alligators Don't Eat Yankees

...and Other Fantasies for Yankees and Southerners Alike

Written & Jud

GW00648970

Published by:
Watermarks Publishing
St. Simons Island, GA

ISBN: 0-9643659-1-X

Library of Congress Catalog Card Number:
96-060339

I

To Kit,
My Favorite Yankee

FOREWORD

The purpose of this book is twofold.

While the animosities engendered by the Civil War have long disappeared, fun loving Southerners still like to pull Yankee legs every now and then. Yankees, at least those with a sense of humor, stand ever ready to respond with the tweaking of a Southern nose whenever they get a chance. It is all a delightful game, enjoyed by all contestants. This book seeks to join the fray -- on both sides.

The book's second purpose is to provide comfort to Yankees living in the Golden Isles. There are more of them now than there were just a few years ago, but they are still in the minority. Like any minority, they suffer anxieties of identity and harbor pangs of insecurity. They worry their children, growing up in the midst of Southerners, will lose their sense of Yankeeism.

These fears are not unfounded. Not long ago I met a little Yankee boy, barely eight years old, who said to me as we shook hands, "How y'all doing, sir?"

His parents, who hail from New York City, were beside themselves with despair. Not only was their offspring talking like a Southerner, he was saying "sir"! For three generations on either side of the family, not a single ancestor had said "sir" to anyone without being forced to do so by some sergeant or other disgusting symbol of authority.

Hopefully, this book will alert Yankees to such risks. Unfortunately, it will not help that poor little New York boy, but I can alleviate his parents' grief by predicting he will eventually outgrow the affliction -- particularly if they get him back up to New York.

Judson J. Conner

INTRODUCTION

"Laugh and the world laughs with you, cry and you cry alone". There's no doubt that this old saying is true, and we all prefer sunshine to rain.

The ability to make people laugh is an art form, not unlike music or painting - a God given talent that only a few people have the good fortune of sharing.

Spoken humor is probably the less difficult form. Stand-up comedians, folks who can tell a joke without blowing the punch line have an easier time than the writer. They have props that they can depend on to enhance their humor. The comedian has a whole array of facial expressions that help set the scene. Remember Jack Benny and his famous "stare"? The audience sees the comedian and is in the mood to laugh long before he tells his joke. They enjoy his antics along with his humor.

Not so the writer. He is there alone, without a stage, without a "live" audience, faced with an unknown reader. Yet through his writing he has to reach this unknown person, lift his mood, make him laugh.

And writer Jud Conner does just this. He takes his talent and brilliant imagination into everyday life, into ordinary situations and finds the humorous side of whatever he sees.

In this book, with tongue in cheek, he explores the South and its people, poking gentle fun at our idiosyncrasies, our habits and our way of life and at the same time also tweaking Yankee noses. He brings his readers a chuckle whether they are Yankee or Southerner.

Settle down with this book, *Alligators Don't Eat Yankees*. It's a book you can dip into whether you have ten minutes to spare or an hour. Let Jud share with you his humorous viewpoint of this corner of the world.

Elise J. Permar, *Editor*

III

TABLE OF CONTENTS

1. ALLIGATORS

Yankees are not particularly fond of alligators. Over the years I have seen numerous alligator handlers, but not a single one of them was a Yankee. This is because Yankees stay as far away from alligators as possible.

Yankee unease over alligators has not been over-looked by Georgians, who delight in spinning alligator tales to terrorize their friends from the North. Most of these stories are false. For example:

Alligators cannot really smell fear, nor do they lurk in the surf of local beaches sniffing for their next meal. This misconception explains why local beaches are never crowded, at least not with Yankees.

It is also untrue that alligators eat only Yankees. Alligators are just as likely to eat a Southerner as a Yankee. In fact, there is some question as to whether alligators can differentiate between Yankees and Southern-ers. Recent studies suggest they cannot. However, all the studies were conducted using Florida alligators, and it is common knowledge that Georgia alligators are much smarter than Florida alligators.

In reality, alligators do not eat people at all -- a fact Yankees should find comforting. They may snap up a stray dog or cat, but they leave people strictly alone. Among their other redeeming qualities is the fact that alligator mothers are most protective of their eggs. Father may eat the young ones once they hatch, but at least the wee ones enter the world amidst the protective aura of motherly love.

Alligator experts assure us alligators are really quite timid and will retreat when approached by a determined man. I have never been determined enough to try this out, but I have no reason to doubt it.

One of the few places where an alligator may appear in the neighborhood of human endeavor is on an isolated golf course which offers nice grassy spots for sunbathing. Needless to say, the appearance of an alligator on a green results in a certain amount of congestion.

Southern golfers take the whole thing in stride and immediately start a discussion over who will move forward to shoo away the intruder. No Yankee ever takes part in these discussions. Any Yankee member of a foursome coming upon a basking alligator is long gone before the discussion gets started.

Eventually one of the Southern golfers volunteers to go back and call the Georgia Fish and Game Department, which dispatches a warden to take care of the problem. While they are waiting, the growing band of delayed golfers swap alligator stories and explain to one another why is is best to leave the shooing away to the Georgia Fish and Game Department.

When the warden arrives, armed with a noose on the end of a long pole, he deftly resolves the problem in no time at all. You see, all Georgia Fish and Game employees are trained to handle alligators.

None of the employees are Yankees.

2. BICYCLES

I was delighted to see St. Simons Island upgrade and expand its fine network of bicycle paths, and I know I am joined by a goodly number of Yankees, and Southerners too, in these sentiments. Particularly appreciative were the considerable number of senior path users, or elderbikers, found here in the Golden Isles.

Unlike the legions of retired Floridians who clutter streets and boardwalks perched on three wheel tricycles for adults, our elderbikers charge up and down intrepidly on real bicycles. And their level of skill is quite awesome.

The younger members of our society tend to overlook the skill required to ride an eldercycle. You see, an elderbike tends to wobble whenever it meets another bicycle, and this can make for a heart-stopping experience. It is particularly hair-raising when two elderbikes meet. This is when the skill factor comes into play. The idea is for the approaching elderbikers to synchronize their wobbles in such a way that one is jigging to starboard as the other jags to port.

It is not an easy skill to master. I find it helps to speed up when I meet a fellow elderbiker. The added speed tends to abate the wobbling somewhat, and it also constricts the time of danger, i.e.: I get the moment of terror over with faster. Of course the added speed appreciably increases one's energy and makes the thought of impact all the more hideous, but, on balance, I figure the degradation of terror outweighs the increase in hideousness. Besides, I wear a bicycle helmet.

In addition to the synchronized wobble, there are other techniques for meeting elderbikes which have been adopted by the cyclists on St. Simons and Jekyll Island. They range from riding off the path and cringing behind the nearest tree to the simple expedient of closing one's eyes.

I know a large woman who uses this latter method quite successfully. By riding in the middle of the path and closing her eyes well before she gets to the point of probable impact, she gives the approaching cyclist plenty of time to react. Most of them prudently adopt the cringe-behind-a-tree course of action, and I have never seen her actually collide with anyone. But I have often wondered what would happen if she met another eye-closer.

Normally, passing bikers in the Golden Isles speak to each other. It is a nice custom. However, to pursue it safely one should know when to speak. The one who initiates the greeting, the "helloer," experiences no difficulty, but the "helloee" can suddenly lose his (or her) concentration if not expecting the greeting. This is particularly hard on newly-arrived Yankees who are unaccustomed to being spoken to by strangers.

Depending on where it occurs, the loss of concentration by an elderbiker "helloee" can lead to a harrowing experience. The elderbike swerves back and forth alarmingly as its rider tries to think of a proper response, and wobble synchronization goes all to pieces. Realizing this, I like to hold my initial "hello" until I am right beside the approaching elderbiker. This allows me to be clear of danger by the time the quivering begins.

Most of the problems outlined above have been solved, or at least alleviated, by the widening of the bicycle paths on St. Simons Island. So all you Yankees out there who are not quite ready to join the Sarasota trike parade, get yourself a two wheeler and come to the Golden Isles.

4

3. CONFEDERATE MONEY

Of all the pitfalls awaiting the unsuspecting Yankee in Coastal Georgia, few are as cruel as the money exchange rate scam practiced by a certain souvenir dealer who has a small shop along a seldom traveled inland highway. Take warning and stay away from him.

You will recognize this establishment by the official-looking money exchange schedule posted inconspicuously in the window. It records the current exchange rate between the dollar and various other currencies, and heading the list is the notation: 1 CD = 1.56 YD.

The average Yankee who drops by to buy a stuffed alligator or genuine coon skin hat seldom notices the sign. Even if he did, it would be meaningless to him. He does not discover its significance until he gets ready to pay the bill. What it means is: One Confederate dollar is worth a bit over one and a half Yankee dollars.

The proprietor explains all this and claims all the prices in the store are marked in Confederate dollars. This means the ten dollars worth of merchandise will cost you $15.60 -- in Yankee dollars.

THIS IS A SCAM. Take heed, my fellow Yankees. I have researched the matter and find there is no difference between the Confederate dollar and the Yankee dollar. This means you should pay no more than the marked price for Southern goods, whether they are marked in CD or YD.

As soon as I discovered the truth about the dollar, I went back to that inland souvenir shop to confront the scam artist. He did not remember me, and I cleverly trapped him into making his false bid by purchasing a toy replica of a Confederate soldier that whistled Dixie when you wound up its left ear. I paid the $13.95 bill with a hundred dollar Yankee note, and when he tried to shortchange me I threatened to call the law down upon his thieving head.

Well, I want you to know, he immediately shifted into full retreat and agreed to give me back the full change. He only had about a quarter of the amount in Yankee dollars, but he made up the rest in Confederate money. He also threw in a pink plastic lawn flamingo for free, just to prove his good will.

So once again, my friends, Justice triumphed over evil. It is nice to know the guys in the white hats still win now and then.

However, I am sorry to report the victory had its dark side. The soldier's ear broke off soon after I got home so he no longer whistles Dixie, and the flamingo turned out to be made of cardboard. I have also experienced some trouble in spending those Confederate dollars.

It seems all the business establishments and banks up and down the Georgia Coast are so used to doing business with Yankees, they are reluctant to take their own money. I may have to go all the way to Atlanta and look up the bank that issued those dollars in order to get them converted.

4. COTTAGES

Newly-arrived Yankees should include on their initial round of visits the fascinating Millionaire Village on Jekyll Island where megabuck mansions were called cottages. These "cottages" are hard for the average Yankee to swallow. Up in Yankee land a cottage is a small dwelling. It may be neat and pretty. It can be cozy and inviting. But it is always small.

The first thought that crosses a Yankee's mind as he gazes in awe at the enormous Jekyll Island "cottages" is that their owners must have hit upon a gimmick to hoodwink the Internal Revenue Service. However, this is not so. The experts tell us they were called cottages -- instead of mansions -- because they contained no kitchens. The owners all took their meals at the Club House.

Whether enlightened or not, the average visitor goes away regarding the Jekyll cottages as relics of a bygone day. But he is wrong. Grand cottages are still very much alive and flourishing. To find them, one has only to visit Sea Island, which is laiterally covered with them.

These Sea Island homes, all known locally as cottages, are every bit as large and elegant as their Jekyll Island counterparts. And unlike their namesakes, they have kitchens and a full range of indoor plumbing. At least I think they do. I have never actually been inside one to see for myself, but I have a friend in real estate who claims they have running water, baths, and even flush toilets. I believe her.

I have no idea why these grand homes on Sea Island are called cottages, although I suspect a certain amount of "me-tooism" is involved. Whatever the reason behind their names, these cottages provide the imaginative Yankee an excellent opportunity to impress his Southern friends along the Georgia coast. All he needs to do is retain a small vacation house up north. A cabin in the woods of Maine or Michigan will do. Then he drops into his conversation every now and then the comment, "We have a cottage back up north ...." Immediately all Southern minds within hearing snap to attention and envision a Yankee version of one of the Sea Island cottages. It is amazing how much respect can be gleaned from that simple comment.

Needless to say, the reverse does not hold true. If a Sea Islander goes up to Yankee land and brags about his cottage, the best he can hope for is a polite yawn. If the owner of southern real estate wants to impress Yankees, he must call his house a plantation.

At one time a plantation consisted of a sizable tract of land and a large house. But over the years the name has been applied by real estate agents to ever-smaller parcels of land and ever-shrinking houses until now a one bedroom bungalow on a quarter acre of swampland qualifies.

Happily, stay at home Yankees do not know this. For them, the word "plantation" conjures up visions of wide verandas, magnolias, Scarlett O'Hara, and Colonel Sanders sitting in a rocking chair lighting cigars with twenty dollar bills.

5. SPANISH MOSS

A newcomer Yankee finds many wonderful and mysterious things in this land of the Golden Isles. Surely not least of these mysteries is how Spanish moss gets hung way up there in the topmost branches of the live oak trees. If he reads up on the elusive gray moss, the Yankee finds it draws its food and water from the air and does not harm its host tree. If he picks up a piece lying on the ground and takes it home for closer examination, as most Yankees do, he also discovers it harbors a whole host of tiny bug critters. But still he has no clue as to how it gets up in the trees.

If the Yankee is naive enough to ask a Southerner about it, he will receive a wide range of answers. One of them holds that the moss is the waste material passed by squirrels feeding on a combination of pecan nuts and unripe Georgia peaches. Another insists that marsh fairies rise up out of the Marshes of Glynn to adorn the trees on the eve of Confederate Memorial Day. When I first arrived in the area I immediately rejected that first explanation. I was sophisticated enough to know Georgia peaches did not grow well on the coastal plain, but it took a night long vigil on the eve of Memorial Day before I realized the fairies story was also a hoax.

After doing some serious research, I finally found the answer to the question. Spanish moss is hung by hand.

Each coastal Georgia county has a special agency for draping moss. It is usually located in the tourist bureau, but may be found in the environmental department or as a separate entity. Other states use various combinations of ladders, poles, and hydraulic hoists to accomplish the job, but in Georgia the task is performed by members of an Irish American family named O'Rangu, who have pretty much cornered the moss-hanging market. This is because long ago some stray mutant struck a pregnant O'Rangu woman, and since that date every second son of O'Rangu mothers has been born with retractable toenails and fingernails. This enables a properly-endowed O'Rangu to scamper up and down trees like a squirrel and even run upside down under branches.

9

Carrying sacks of Spanish moss shoots grown at the State Moss Nursery located near Jesup, a Georgia moss hanger (GMH) can replenish an astonishing number of live oak trees in just one night. It is said that Dan, a legendary O'Rangu GMH, can service  all the trees on Jekyll Island in a single night.

The governor of Florida has tried for years to hire an O'Rangu moss hanger, but they have remained loyal to Georgia, thereby forcing Florida to rely on ladders and long poles to adorn its trees. All you have to do is look at a Florida live oak to truly appreciate the O'Rangu family.

By and large, O'Rangu family members are very modest people who shun publicity. They only work in the dead of night and when not among the branches of live oak trees, they wear normal street clothes and pass as average, run-of-the-mill, ungifted people. In fact, the only way to positively identify a GMH is to examine his feet. He is not able to completely retract the toenails on his big toes, although by wearing shoes he is able to conceal this characteristic.

Only on rare occasions does a practicing GMH slip up and show his claws. One might forget and spear an hors d'oeuvre at a cocktail party, or perhaps sneak a scratch while suffering from a persistent itch, or maybe use an extended nail to fish a foreign object out of his ear during a Savannah St. Patrick's Day Parade. But it does not happen very often.

Even an alert observer seldom spots a careless GMH. However, there is a way to discover one if you are really interested in doing so. GMH's work only at night, but they spend much of the daylight hours checking the tops of live oak trees to detect thinning areas of Spanish moss. So if you ever see a man gazing at the top of a live oak tree, just go up to him and ask him to take off his shoes. If he refuses, you can be sure he is an O'Rangu — perhaps even the legendary Dan himself.

6. HEY!

Language differences can make it hard on a Yankee visiting the Golden Isles for the first time. He has no trouble with communications when it comes to the really important things, like how much he has to pay for food and lodging and souvenirs. Most Southerners understand Yankee, particularly when it is spoken in reference to money. The problems arise because most Yankees cannot understand Southern.

Over time the difficulties are ameliorated, because most of the differences are rooted in pronunciation. As the Yankee ear becomes southernized it acquires the ability to pass the correct information to the Yankee brain. But it is not all a question of pronunciation. Some words have different meanings, and they can be most perplexing -- unless a kindly soul like me takes the time to explain them.

One such stumbling block is the word "hey."

To the average Yankee the word is an attention-gaining expression, as a mailman might use in speaking to a dog, "Hey, leggo my leg!" It can also be coupled with the word "there" as Rosemary Clooney once did. "Hey there, you with the stars in your eyes ...." But whether standing alone or coupled, "hey" signals to the Yankee that something more is coming, and he stops whatever he is doing to listen for the follow on.

All this can lead to great confusion along the Georgia Coast, because down here, "hey" does not mean "hey." It means "hello." Consider the Yankee who telephones a Southern friend. "Hey," answers the Southerner and the Yankee concentrates and waits for the rest of the sentence. Finally there is another "hey," a bit louder this time, and the Yankee realizes he is going to have say something or his end of the wire is going to collapse. So he does, and it is usually something like, "So what do you want?" This strikes the Southerner as pretty stupid, since the Yankee initiated the call, and he is likely to tell him so.

By this time each party is convinced the other one is an idiot, and it will be a long time before that friendship blossoms into one of mutual trust. All this can be avoided if Yankees will just learn to say "hey" right back when greeted by a Southerner.

You might think the same sort of misunderstanding results if the circumstances are reversed and the Yankee initiates the exchange by saying "hello," but this is not the case. Southerners living in the Golden Isles have met enough Yankees to know very well that "hello" means "hey."

7. BIRD MAN OF THE ALTAMAHA

It is difficult to find anything to complain about in the Golden Isles, but some of my Yankee friends have found a pet peeve: birds -- specifically black birds and cow birds that hang around the outdoor eating establishments. Several Yankee citizens have had tidbits snatched off their plates, and one lady lost a barely-chewed piece of gum she had neatly parked on the edge of a saucer while she ate.

I tend to sympathize with my Yankee friends, since I too have had to match wits with the feathery filchers, but having researched the matter, I find there is a logical explanation for the bird behavior. It all started with one Tylor T. Allaguard, a most gifted bird trainer who was known as the Bird Man of the Altamaha.

During the 1920's and '30's, Tylor roamed the back country of Georgia along the banks of the Altamaha, trapping, taming, and training wild birds. Clark Gable's pet Blue Jay was a graduate of the Tylor Training School, and the talking egret Admiral Byrd carried with him for company to the South Pole had learned the art of conversation from Tylor.

Tylor derived his natural talents from his grandfather, Yancy Allaguard, who was the platoon leader of the one and only pigeon platoon on the rolls of the Confederate Army. They flew brilliantly for Robert E. Lee from Antietam to Cold Harbor. Here, while grounded by bad weather, they were surprised and captured by a unit of hungry Yankees. Lieutenant Allaguard was paroled, but the rest of the platoon was eaten. Yancy never forgot, nor forgave, this Yankee atrocity, and neither did his grandson.

With the advent of affordable automobiles and the growth of paved roads, great droves of Yankees began motoring down U.S. Route 1 in the decades prior to World War II to populate Florida and throw picnic trash along the roads in Georgia. Alarmed, Tylor conceived a plan designed to both protect the Georgia countryside and strike a mighty blow for the Confederacy on behalf of the devoured pigeon platoon. Appropriately, he chose birds as his agents of revenge.

Tylor's plan was to create an army of hungry birds to descend on all Yankees eating anywhere in the state of Georgia and so disrupt their meals that they would retreat back up north or, better still, starve to death before they could reach Florida. For several years he taught his bevy of birds to pluck sandwiches from fingers, tip over pitchers of Koolaid, and stomp up and down through mashed potatoes. The birds were programmed to ignore Southern diners. This was accomplished by placing assorted Southern foods -- grits, corn bread, collard greens, etc.-- on metal plates carrying a mild electric charge. It only took a few jolts to turn the birds into real experts on Southern cuisine.

Tylor was fully aware that at best he could only train a few hundred birds, but he anticipated his protégés would pass on, through example, their anti-Yankee antics to future generations. Birds are great imitators, and, as it turned out, Tylor was right.

When Tylor had trained seven or eight hundred birds, he distributed them along Route 1, the Florida border, and at various places where Yankees tended to congregate, such as Sea Island and under huge shade trees. Immediately they went to work and everything transpired just as Tylor had planned. But there was a catch. The Yankees were delighted with the birds.

Instead of shooing away their detractors, the Yankees welcomed them. The feathered fiends provided the only friendly encounters Yankees found in Georgia, and they were only too glad to share their food with them. Instead of becoming scenes of fear and panic, picnic sites along Georgia highways became pockets of happy Yankees and fat, contented birds. Tylor was crushed. He spent the rest of his life trying to develop a black bird capable of carrying a hand grenade and died a broken man in 1938. But his dream lives on.

Those pesky birds which bother patrons of open air restaurants on the Golden Isles are descendants of the Tylor birds. Of course, much has changed over the past sixty years. Picnics have become fewer, but outdoor dining establishments have multiplied. Time has dulled the birds' ability to differentiate between northern and southern dishes -- very few grit bowls carry electric charges nowadays --,so Southerners are as likely to be the target of an aerial assault as Yankees are.

Several attempts have been made to thwart the pesky birds, but for one reason or another, all have failed. One man from Jekyll Island fashioned a hat with a large stuffed owl perched on top of it to frighten off the birds. This it did, but it also frightened off waitresses, and drew hostile stares from the other customers.

Another ingenious try was made by a lon- time resident of St. Simons who trained a cat to ride quietly and unobtrusively in a shoulder holster under his coat. The idea was for the cat to stick its head out when a bird approached, thereby assuring a bird-free repast. However, the cat carrier failed to anticipate what the cat would do when it peered out to find a bird perched on a salt shaker barely two feet from its nose. On its first, and only, appearance at an outside dining facility, the cat exploded out of the shoulder holster and went romping from one table to the next chasing birds. Then it discovered the seafood restaurant served cooked food which tasted much better than raw birds. It had devoured several platters of haddock before it was scooped up by the manager and, along with its master, tossed out into the street. Having birds stomping through mashed potatoes is one thing, having a cat do it is quite another.

While all anti-bird efforts have failed so far, this is no reason for us to give up. Surely Yankee ingenuity can come up with a solution. I will be happy to try out any suggestion, as long as it does not

Involve owls or cats.

8. COVERED BRIDGES

Visiting Yankees are not apt to find many things to remind them of home along the Georgia coast, but there is one exception to this rule. On St. Simons Island, just off Kings Way at the entrance to the Island Club, stands a covered bridge. Homesick Yankees have been known to burst into tears at the unexpected sight.

Not all Yankees appreciate the significance of a covered bridge, but those from New England do. Many of these far north Yankees are gripped by a mystical force exerted by covered bridges and sugar maple trees. Wherever they are in the world, once a year they must seek out a covered bridge or sugar maple tree to renew their spirits and replenish their sense of Yankeeism.

The existence of the Island Club bridge offers a welcome alternative to the long pilgrimage up I-95, thereby saving Golden Isles Yankees a bunch of time and money and alleviating traffic congestion.

Now it is true the St. Simons covered bridge is somewhat different from the ones in New England. The purist is quick to point out it lacks the internal arch, wide beams, and thick boards of the true Yankee bridge. But a covered bridge is a covered bridge, as far as I am concerned, and all but the ultra-orthodox Yankees tend to agree with me.

Not only does the bridge offer Golden Isles Yankees a chance to drive back and forth over the structure, it also contains two covered pedestrian lanes where they can linger to indulge in a bit of nostalgia and drop a spattering of homesick tears into the water below. These pedestrian walk-ways also make it easier for distraught Yankees to hurl themselves over the side. Not many New England covered bridges offer such convenience. In fact, it is next to impossible to jump off Vermont or New Hampshire covered bridges, because they are all enclosed.

In spite of its facilitating structural features, the St. Simons covered bridge has not proven popular as a suicide platform. This is probably because a jumper would have a tough time drowning in the shallow lagoon lying beneath it. A face full of mud is the most he could reasonably expect from his efforts. Besides, no Yankee in his right mind, suicidal or otherwise, would jump into a dark body of water in any state where there was an alligator population.

As far as I know, no Yankee has ever attempted suicide from that bridge, or anywhere else in the Golden Isles, for that matter. I suppose all this just goes to prove that once a Yankee falls under the spell of these live oaks and warm coastal breezes, he becomes a contented Yankee, and his longing for northern climes fades away. He may visit the north in the summer, but winter finds him back on the Georgia Coast. All he has to do to banish lingering pangs of nostalgia is turn on the television weather channel.

9. SOUTHERN DOGS

Yankees are often puzzled by the sign appearing in front of some Southern kennels: Pedigreed Southern Dogs. Is there really a difference between Southern dogs and Yankee dogs? And if so, how can you tell one from the other? The answer to the first question is: Yes, there is. And to the second: I am about to tell you.

Differentiating between Yankee and Southern dogs is not an easy task. Unlike their human masters, Southern and Yankee dogs sound alike -- except for the Georgia Bulldog, of course. Therefore, one must look to subtle behavioral differences to properly identify a Southern dog. Their inherent urge to hunt all night makes Southern dogs prone to sleeping all day, and they always choose the shade of a big tree in which to sleep, even in the winter time. And, by and large, the Southern dog takes a much more relaxed view of the world than does his Yankee cousin. Yankee canines will spring from a deep sleep into a yapping challenge at the slightest noise. But the snoozing Southerner merely opens one eye and glances around to see if the noise is worth getting up for. It seldom is.   ⁄

This does not mean Southern dogs cannot be trained as watch dogs. They can and are. In fact they take to biting Yankees quite readily, although additional training is required for them to work up an anger over a Southern trespasser.

Southern dogs are outdoor dogs. If brought inside a house, the Southern dog feels very ill at ease and is likely to treat the inside of the house exactly as he would the outdoors. I have heard Southern wives claim this is a learned trait, since their husbands do exactly the same thing. However, so far as I know, there is no truth to this complaint. I have never seen a Southern husband try to bury a bone under the rug or drink out of the toilet bowl.

Southern male dogs always lift their legs on the south side of trees and fire hydrants. No one has yet come up with a logical explanation for this phenomenon, or at least not a scientific one, but it has enabled many a hunter lost and without a compass to find his way to safety by letting his dog point the way.

Southern dogs are able to contract the soles of their paws to form suction cups. This foot cupping ability allows them to ride with apparent ease in the back of pickup trucks traveling down country roads at 164 miles per hour.

All Southern dogs like to hunt. Just one whiff of a raccoon or opossum and the little critters are off in howling pursuit. Now it is true, certain Yankee dogs like to hunt too. It is not unusual to hear a Yankee beagle or basset hound baying in hot pursuit of a woodland prey, but you never hear a Yankee Pekingese doing it. To find a baying Pekingese, you have to come down South.

You are probably wonding why dogs with all these great characteristics have not been imported for sale in the North. Well, it has been tried, but, unfortunately, a blanket of snow has a decidedly adverse affect on the Southern dog. After spending just one year in Yankee Land, the Southern dog has shivered away all itsSouthern characteristics and is doomed to be a Yankee for rest of its life.

This sad transformation does not work in reverse, however. Yankee dogs coming south remain Yankee dogs, and over the years a great many of them have invaded the South and sullied the blood line of the true Southern canine. The Southern Kennel Klub (SKK) is just now beginning to address the problem, and while much has been accomplished, much still remains to be done. A spokesman for the SKK explains that the canine carpetbaggers have just about taken over St. Simons and Jekyll Islands, and a concerted effort is currently under way to round up the few remaining Southern dogs on the islands and take them to a sheltered area deep in the Georgia interior.

You can help in this noble effort. Now that you know how to identify a Southern dog, if you find one running loose, pick him up and get word to an SKK member who will dispatch a rescue team to pick him up. But while you are waiting, do not take him into your house.

10. SPANISH GRAVES

When a Yankee first comes to the Golden Isles, he finds many strange and fascinating things to tweak his curiosity. Most local people are happy to provide him with accurate information, but there are some who enjoy pulling Yankee legs. I discovered this the hard way when I asked about the little orange and yellow flags adorning the lawns on St. Simons Island.

We were just leaving the site of the Battle of Bloody Marsh at the time, and I was told they marked the site of Spanish graves. My Southern friend went on to explain they were placed there each year by the Spanish Legion, on Spanish Memorial Day, to mark the final resting place of Spanish soldiers killed at Bloody Marsh.

I had no reason to doubt this explanation. After all, the Spanish are a very compassionate, caring people. But then I began noticing Spanish graves all over the Island. In fact, there were enough of them to hold the whole Spanish army.

Eventually I discovered these flags do not mark Spanish graves at all, but indicate the location of underground utility conduits. But still nagging questions remained. I have yet to see any workmen using the information furnished by the flags, nor have I ever seen anyone placing or removing the flags. They just seem to appear out of nowhere, and then vanish just as mysteriously a few days later.

After giving the mystery some thought, I believe I have found the answer. I figure each utility company has on its payroll an expert on underground utility line location. Since his services are rarely required, he has other tasks to perform during normal work hours. But the art of locating underground utility lines is a perishable one, and those licensed to perform it can maintain their proficiency only through continuous practice.

Because of his other duties, the locator of utility lines underground, or LULU, as he is known among his fellow utility workers, finds time to practice his craft only during off-duty hours. Every few days he gathers up a shopping bag full of orange and yellow flags and sets off in the dark of night to probe the lawns of St. Simons and plant his markers. Then, a few nights later, when he begins to run low on flags, he retraces his tracks and retrieves them.

Such dedication most certainly deserves our admiration and support. I do hope you will all remember your local LULU whenever you plug in an electric appliance or turn on a water faucet.

11. OLYMPIC TIDDLYWINKS

Yankee entrepreneurs have played important parts in the history of the Golden Isles, but few were more enterprising, or less known, than Pheneous P. Pilfenheimer. According to rumor, he appeared in the area soon after Atlanta had been named the site of the 1996 Summer Olympics. He had a vision. Since his vision carried with it certain monetary advantage, it was immediately embraced by several local merchants.

The vision called for locating the 1996 Olympic tiddlywink contests on St. Simons and Jekyll Islands.

Pheneous explained that tiddlywink professionals tended to avoid the spotlight and preferred holding their contests in quiet settings, far from the distractions of large cities. St. Simons was the perfect site. It not only provided a quiet setting, it was close enough to Atlanta to allow the contestants to participate in opening and closing Olympic ceremonies.

It all sounded very logical, and Pheneous P. Pilfenheimer was obviously the man who could pull it off. He modestly admitted he was well known in international tiddlywink circles and was once the New England tiddlywinks champion. Indeed, he would probably have become national champion had he not injured his flipping thumb in a semifinal match with Chicago's Illinois Slim. Slim went on to claim the title.

The planning was done in secrecy to avoid interference by the Atlanta Olympic committee. Match sites were allocated according to money contributed or pledged to the project. Men's singles were to be flipped at a resort motel on Jekyll, women's doubles in Redfern Village, and so on. When at last plans and contributions were sufficiently advanced to make the critical presentation to the International Olympic Committee, Pheneous volunteered to take on the task, with a stopover along the way to touch base with the International Tiddlywinks Commission in Paris.

Several of the project backers were on hand at the airport to see him off. Armed with plans, pledges, and a roll of big bills to buy gifts for influential committee members, Pheneous waved good bye, stepped into the plane, and was never seen again.

Fear that Pheneous had met with foul play in some back alley of Paris gave way to anger when one of the project backers stumbled on the fact that tiddlywinks competition was not part of the Summer Olympics. At a hastily-called meeting, the duped merchants decided the chances of finding Pheneous and that roll of big bills was very remote, indeed. They also decided the whole thing best be forgotten as soon as possible. Everyone took a pledge of secrecy which has remained remarkably intact to this day.

I do not know for sure this story is true. But I do know it is impossible to buy a set of tournament tiddlywinks on the islands of St. Simons or Jekyll. And I am told if you ask for such a set at certain business establishments, you are very likely to get thrown out on your ear.

12. SNAKE IDENTIFICATION

Yankees are naturally apprehensive about snakes. There are snakes up north, of course, even poisonous snakes, but not in the number they are found in Georgia.

Because of their aversion to the reptile, Yankees are likely to keep strictly on paved areas. This is a great pity, for much of Georgia's charm is located in her marshlands and sprawling pine forests.

This Yankee fear is based mostly on ignorance. A knowledge of how to identify poisonous snakes goes far in dispelling apprehension. I am happy to be able to provide the rudiments of this knowledge here and now. The information proffered was accrued by way of intensive research and a visit to Bubba Burke's Reptile Farm and Scientific Research Center.

First of all, snakes are very beneficial creatures and should be protected. Poisonous snakes make up but a small portion of the overall Georgia snake population. In fact, there are only three varieties of poisonous snakes you are likely to encounter in Georgia, and since all three are pit vipers, they are easily identified.

To determine if a snake is a pit viper, grasp him firmly just behind the ears, or where the ears would be if he had ears, and hold his head about one foot from your face at eye level. Look for a pair of pits, or holes, located just forward of and below the eyes. If you locate them, you know the snake you are holding is poisonous, but you still do not know which kind of snake it is.

You determine the specie of snake through the process of elimination. First note the color of his mouth. You need not worry about how to get him to open his mouth. If you have him firmly grasped behind the ears, he will have his mouth open. If that mouth is white, you have a water moccasin, or cotton-mouth, as he is sometimes called.

If his mouth is not white, check the end of his tail for a rattle. If there is one there, he is a rattlesnake. If he has no rattle and his mouth is not white, then he is probably a copperhead, in which case he will undoubtedly be a deep copper color.

Now wasn't that simple? Henceforth you can go tramping about the back lands of Georgia without fear of running across an unidentified snake. Happy trails to you.

But hold on! My wife, who functions as a low budget proof-reader, has just read this over and brought up a picky point which I probably should address. She wants to know how you go about firmly grasping that snake behind where his ears should be.

Well, frankly, I do not know. However, I will make another trip to Bubba Burke's Reptile Farm and Scientific Research Center to find the answer.

In the meantime, just concentrate on those pits.

13. TRAFFIC LIGHTS

If you are a Yankee who spends part of the year on St. Simons Island, you have probably noticed the peculiar timing of the island traffic lights.

As you approach a light which is green, no matter how far back you first spot it, it will stay green until you have almost reached it, at which time it turns red, and stays red for several minutes. On the other hand, if it is red when you first see it, it stays red until you have reached the intersection and stopped, no matter how slowly you approach it. And when you are in a line of cars turning left, the left turn signal stays on only long enough to clear the the cars in front of you, then ZIP, it is red.

For some period of time I thought I was the victim of chance of poorly timed lights. Then while riding with some Southern friends, I began to realize the lights worked normally for them. In fact, the lights seemed to turn green whenever they approached. I immediately donned my investigative cloak and sallied forth on behalf of all Yankees to get to the bottom of this flagrant violation of Yankee rights.

Assisted by information provided by a Yankee mole planted deep within the inner circles of Georgia officialdom, I discovered it is all part of an ongoing program to discourage outsiders from settling in the Golden Isles. However the harassments are not directed toward Yankees alone, but are targeted against anyone who is from out of state. It all hinges on license plates.

You have probably noticed that Georgia is one of the few states that issues only one license plate. This allows for quick and accurate identification of out of state cars which, in turn, provides a trigger for a whole host of activity designed to frustrate visitors. Traffic light control is just one of them.

Initially, control wires were strung from the traffic lights to nearby trees where small individuals were concealed high up among the branches. Armed with a set of binoculars, the controllers spotted the approach of non-Georgia cars and manipulated the lights accordingly. Look closely high up in the trees located near traffic lights and you can still see the remnants of the small seats where they sat.

This method of light control was eventually abandoned as the result of several problems. The little controllers kept falling out of the trees in high winds, and their camouflaged uniforms not only fooled motorists, they fooled birds and squirrels as well. It was difficult to remain motionless and keep one's mind on the job while one's ear was being stuffed with nuts.

Fortunately technology came to the aid of the program, and the tree sitters were replaced by television cameras built right into the traffic lights. With wires leading back to a secret chamber, one individual could sit in front of a bank of monitors, safe from wind and squirrels, and control all the lights of the island. Needless to say, the location of this control center is a closely-guarded secret. I have heard rumors it is in the cellar under the kitchen of the Cloister's five-star restaurant, but I cannot confirm this.

Keeping track of all the Yankees approaching all the lights on St. Simons proved to be a mind-boggling experience. Few were able to hold the position for more than a few weeks at a time, even when they were rotated to the less demanding job of holding warning flags at road construction sites every third day. Eventually a computer was developed to do the job, and this is where the program stands now.

Now that you know what is behind the contrary timing of the island traffic lights, I am sure you are interested in how the system can be beaten. Unfortunately, your options are limited. You can remove or cover up your front license plate, but local policemen are very curious when it comes to missing front license plates on cars registered in any state but Georgia. It does not pay to upset the local police.

There is another possible solution for those who have cars with relatively flat hoods. Have someone sit on the hood and casually cover the front license plate with her feet when you approach a light. This method also has its drawbacks. I tried it but gave up on it because I got tired of hearing my wife complain, particularly in rainy weather.

Eventually I broke down and got our car registered in Georgia. This did the trick. The lights went back to normal sequencing of red and green, and then I discovered another interesting fact. That computer is a very sophisticated machine, indeed, and if you have a something in that front license plate holder that shows the proper spirit, you are rewarded by having the traffic lights flick on and off in your favor no matter at what speed you approach them. A plate showing a Confederate flag does the trick, and so do plates with various lettering such as "St. Simons Island " and "Down With Yankee Imperialism!"

Realizing the drawbacks of the current system, Georgia scientists are now working on a new generation of computers which will look through the windshield of a car and recognize a Yankee, thereby freeing the system of its dependency on license plates. So far they have not been able to produce a workable model, and best estimates put the breakthrough at least three or four years in the future. In the meantime, just get your cars registered in Georgia.

14. SPORT FISHING

I enjoy fishing, but I cannot understand why fishing is considered a sport. I always considered a sport as being a contest with an uncertain outcome, a test of skills between teams or individuals of comparative abilities. Once a fish enters a contest with an angler, the outcome is very nearly a foregone conclusion.

I have a proposal which will change all this. It introduces a challenging unpredictability which will convert the pastime of fishing into an exciting spectator sport, one that will rival golf in popularity. Successful professional fishermen will become national idols and compete for hefty purses.

Here is the way it will work. Fishermen, as members of teams or as individuals, will wade out waist deep into the ocean to do their fishing. Referees in small boats will pass among them sowing the waters with dead fish, red meat, and fresh blood. Even if sharks do not appear, the potential of their presence will generate much excitement for contestants and spectators alike.

For team competition, winners will be judged by the total number of fish caught by each team during a set period, say an hour. Ties may be resolved by either counting the number of contestants remaining on each team or by holding "sudden death" overtimes.

Generation of prize money should be no problem. Bleachers erected along the shore would hold numerous paying spectators. Television revenues should be considerable, and advertising on billboards constructed atop off-shore rafts would bring in additional revenues. Advertisers will come flocking -- those who sell fishing equipment, band aid companies, manufacturers of wheelchairs and artificial limbs, pharmaceutical distributors of aspirin and other pain killers, etc.

Professional fishing teams will spring up all along the coast: The Saint Simons Slashers, Hilton Head Dodgers, Cape Cod Catchers, etc. Talented performers will be catapulted to stardom, and fans will gather to collect autographs from Stump Stagger and Peg Leg Lagono. The indomitable Hook Higgins will be interviewed by Oprah.

Publicity and heavy money will naturally flow to the pro's, but the wonderful thing about the new Sport Fishing will be its amateur appeal. Economically within reach of just about everyone, it will require no expensive preparation or equipment for beginners.

I confidently predict, once the idea has caught on, that people of all ages will be enjoying the sport. But do not wait until all the good fishing spots are taken. Grab your fishing pole, drop by a local butcher shop for some fresh meat scraps, and head for the beach.

And please let me know when you do this so I can go along to watch.

15. STREETS

Among the confusing things confronting newly-arrived Yankees are the streets of St. Simons Island. The confusion arises from their naming, routing, and marking, all of which suggest the workings of a diabolical mind determined to confound Yankees.

Take, for example, Demere Road. Named for one of Oglethorpe's company commanders, it manages to run both north and south and east and west (twice). Starting out on either end of Demere Road the visitor travels toward the east, and when he gets to the other end he is moving west - - regardless of which end he started on. Few places have a street like that.

In spite of its meandering, the most frustrating thing about Demere Road to the newcomer is its pronunciation. Breaking it into its logical parts, "de" and "mere," the average Yankee pronounces it "demeer." But this is not the pronunciation used by the local inhabitants. They call it "demoray" with the accent on the "ay."

However, those living on the island do not normally correct the newcomer. They raise their eyebrows in patient disgust and let him go right on sounding idiotic, until some kindly soul, like me, comes along to set him straight.

Another worrisome thing about St. Simons streets is their curious habit of changing names without letting anyone know. Kings Way does this.

Starting just east of the causeway, the traveler follows Kings Way through a tunnel of majestic live oaks to the village of St. Simons, then on around the curve of the Island to its end at East Beach. There he discovers he is not on Kings Way at all, but rather on Ocean Boulevard. Retracing his steps to find where the transformation took place, he works his way all the way back to the causeway without finding the point where one street turned into another. This is because only the far ends of streets are marked on St. Simons, presumably a measure designed to take pressure off the treasury and confuse Yankees.

31

Another name-changing thoroughfare is Mallory Street. Running north from the village, it swings around Mallory Park and travels eastward to Demere, at which point it is Proctor Street. The change in names apparently takes place somewhere in the vicinity of Mallory Park, but don't quote me on this.

Finally there is Frederica Road, running southeast and south from Fort Frederica to Demere, where it quietly becomes Plantation Way and continues south until it is swallowed up by the golfing greens of Retreat Plantation. No sign marks the point of change, so most people pay no attention to Plantation Way. They just keep driving along the west flank of the airport on Frederica Road, whether the maps and street namers say so or not.

The whole thing smacks of a conspiracy to confuse Yankees and discourage immigration. But there has been retaliation.

Apparently, sometime in the past, some Yankee worked his way into the inner circle of St. Simons street namers and managed to get one of the streets named Sherman, Sherman Avenue to be exact. Now, having a street in Georgia named Sherman is akin to having an Adolf Hitler Avenue in Tel Aviv. How it ever slipped by the south Georgia Political Correctness Committee remains a mystery.

I will not tell you just where Sherman Avenue is located. I have been asked to keep its whereabouts a secret lest those who live on the street suffer retaliation from the Daughters of the Confederacy. But it is worth looking up. Hint: start looking on the southeast quadrant of the island between Oaks Drive and Myrtle.

16. WHALES

In case you have not recognized it, that gray blob of concrete splashing around on the south end of St. Simons' Neptune Park is a mama whale and her baby. I want all you Golden Isles Yankees to scurry on down to see it, if you have not done so already. I figure this is the only mama whale and calf the average Yankee will ever see, real or otherwise, and it is not something to be passed up.

The St. Simons Chamber of Commerce claims the statue is designed to call attention to the plight of Right Whales that annually traverse the Georgia coast in ever-dwindling number, and to enhance tourism -- not necessarily in that order. It will also enhance the business of conducting whale-watching excursions.

I have always been fascinated by these whale watching excursions and have noticed that those who conduct them do not guarantee a whale will be sighted on a given cruise. I am told by those who know something about migrating whales that this lack of guarantee is no accident, but rather a very wise oversight.

However, whale-watching enthusiasts do not seem to mind. Apparently the exhilarating anticipation experienced on the outbound journey overshadows disappointment suffered on the way back. I have often thought a small serving of spirits would help alleviate the disappointment. Indeed, a small tot of wine might also assist in the spotting of whales, but so far as I know, no such offering is provided. However, none of this matters to me, because my purpose is not to enhance the whale-watching business, but rather to suggest a totally new concept. I offer it, without regard for personal compensation, to any enterprising Yankee out there who might be interested.

The idea is to offer off-coast cruises to see Sam, the St. Simons Sea Monster.

As local sea-faring men will tell you, Sam lives off the coast of Georgia in one of the caves carved into the continental shelf. He is about the size of Sea Island and has a big mouth, long fangs, piercing eyes, and nostrils that snort fire. His diet consists of Right Whales -- which accounts for their dwindling number -- and Coast Guard cutters.

I figure the average tourist would much rather see a sea monster than a Right Whale and would pay considerably more for the chance. And when you come right down to it, his chance of seeing Sam would be just about as great as it is to see a migrating whale. Maybe even better, because I would serve Georgia white lightning instead of wine.

With a little PR assistance, Sam could become a really popular tourist attraction. His fresh-water cousin, the Loch Ness Monster, attracts thousands of tourists, and Chessy, the female monster in Lake Champlain, has turned many a pretty penny for imaginative Yankees.

There is no reason local businesses should not cash in on Sam too. The Chamber of Commerce could put up a statue of Sam, perhaps in the act of eating its two whales, and selling stuffed Sam dolls would make all the local merchants rich. Sam bumper stickers would adorn bumpers, and visitors would flock to buy Sam coloring books and Sam sculptures cranked out by local artists. We could get the Governor to proclaim a "Sam Day," and ....

On second thought, this idea is not for free. I will demand a cut from anyone who develops the concept.

17. COURSE IN YANKEE

Yankees living among the Golden Isles are fortunate inasmuch as they are generally understood wherever they go, at least by merchants and government officials. Many take it all for granted, assuming the familiarity with the Yankee language exhibited by the indigenous population is the natural result of association. Association and usage do play a part -- indeed, Yankees begin to pick up the meaning of some Southern words after being here for a while --,but the real credit goes to the far-sighted Glynn County officials who set up a Yankee language school some years ago.

It all began when the emergency number 911 was adopted. Operators simply could not understand Yankee callers. An ambulance was dispatched in the middle of the night to take care of an ingrown toenail. A police SWAT team was rushed to a St. Simons address to get a cat down from a tree. And on that same night a 911 operator spent half an hour talking a distraught lady through the steps of mouth-to-mouth resuscitation while an ambulance crew rushed to save her husband. The victim turned out to be a choking pet canary named Osebund. Needless to say, the misunderstandings were embarrassing and expensive -- and downright traumatic as far as that poor canary was concerned.

The very next day a school was established to teach 911 operators to understand Yankee. It proved so popular, policemen, firemen, tax collectors, and others who had to deal with Yankees began enrolling. Eventually the school was taken over by private enterprise and significantly expanded by the new owner, a Professor Berlitze. It now offers a variety of specialized disciplines such as Waitress Yankee, Plumber Yankee, Mechanic Yankee, Conversation Yankee, Medical Yankee, Drowning Yankee (for potential lifeguards), and several others. There are also departments which specialize in various Yankee dialects: the Department of New York Yankee, the Department of New England Nasal Studies, Midwestern Inflections, and the Department of Baaston Yankee.

Many of the students take more than one course. I know a plumber who not only can understand what is wrong with Yankee plumbing, he can carry on a conversation in passable Yankee as he fixes it. This gives him a distinct competitive edge over competitors. And there is a local doctor who can diagnose hemorrhoids whether they appear in a New Yorker, Midwesterner, or New England Yankee.

While the school remains primarily focused on the Golden Isles, students from other parts of Georgia, as well as other Southern states also attend. Special courses are conducted for members of the Southern Custom Service (SCS) and the Confederate Information Agency (CIA). The latter students take a long, comprehensive course in understanding Yankee as preparation for their being inserted into key Yankee cities such as Chicago, New York, Philadelphia, and Miami. This is only part of their training, of course, because their cover requires they speak Yankee as well as understand it. Professor Berlitze is quick to point out his school only teaches how to understand Yankee, not to speak it.

In order for a Southerner to speak Yankee without an accent, he must undergo a larynx transplant. This is a very expensive process. The procedure itself is relatively simple, and safe, but Yankee larynxes are very hard to come by. As a rule, Yankees do not part with their larynxes willingly, and the only non-coercive source is the organ donor program carried out by the Georgia Highway Department. Nor is it all that easy to find agents willing to undergo the operation. Living dangerously in a hostile environment for extended periods of time is one thing, coming back home talking like a Yankee is quite another. Most agents are disowned by their families and few are ever able to return to their land of birth even after they retire.

But I digress from the subject at hand. We are speaking here, not of Southerners who can speak Yankee, but of those who can understand Yankee. And there are a great number of them living along the coast of Georgia, thanks mainly to the Glynn County officials and Professor Theodore Berlitze. I call upon all you Yankees to extend to them a hearty cheer and to murmur a "thank you" every time you enter a commercial establishment and see the welcoming sign, "Yankee understood here."

Since the establishment of the Berlitze Yankee Language School, the Golden Isles have become a much more Yankee-friendly place to live. Medical emergencies no longer have to be sent to Miami or New York for treatment, and if a Yankee house catches on fire, there is a good chance it will be saved. And today if you call 911 to get your cat down from a tree, you will no longer be visited by a police SWAT team. Just one policeman will call, and he will give you a citation for improperly using the 911 emergency number.

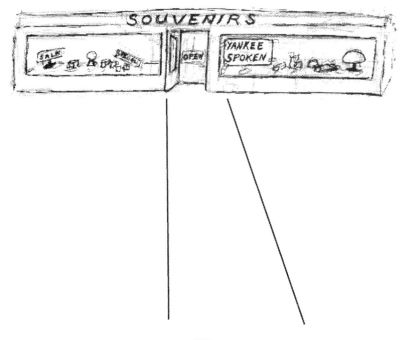

JEKYLL ISLAND SAFARI

Jekyll Island is not exactly overflowing with wildlife. Yankee visitors to the Golden Isles searching for wild animals would do better looking elsewhere, particularly if they are searching for alligators. I know this from personal experience, since I spent the better part of an afternoon making the effort with my grandson, Goober.

It occurred one afternoon when I took Goober and his parents for a sightseeing drive to Jekyll Island. I explained to the steely-eyed gate-keeper who collects the two dollar island parking fee that there would be no need for me to pay, since I was not going to stop, much less park.

The toll taker flashed a big smile and said, "We have such a beautiful island, visitors find it impossible to resist stopping to admire its beauty. Two dollars, please."

I agreed his island was beautiful but informed him I had seen it several times and was sure I could resist the temptation to stop.

The guard sighed, glanced at Goober, and said, "But what if you come across an alligator? Surely you will want to stop for a better look."

"I want to see an alligator," shouted Goober.

"I have never yet seen an alligator anywhere on Jekyll Island," said I, "and I doubt if you have either."

"That is probably because you did not have an alligator map," explained the guard. "Now I have an alligator map right here somewhere, and I will give it to you when you pay your two dollars. Just pull over there while I find it."

"I want to see an alligator," yelled Goober.

There was no sense debating the matter in front of Goober, so I pulled over to the side of the road and went back to continue the argument. The smiling toll taker handed me a copy of the standard strip map given to all visitors. At the the top he had written "alligators" and drawn an arrow in red ink to the the marshy area behind the fishing pier. "Two dollars, sir."

With righteous indignation, I refused to pay two dollars

for that stupid map, but he explained the map was free. "The two dollars are for parking on the island, which you have already done." He gestured toward the car where Gooper was leaning out the window looking for alligators.

I knew I had been had. I paid Smiley the two dollars, took my alligator map, and went off on an alligator safari. Goober's grandmother -- who tends to side with toll takers -- announced that alligator hunting was men's work and she and my daughter-in-law would sit out the hunt at one of the local cocktail lounges. My son, who is a lot like his mother, decided to join them for protection, in case one of the alligators slipped by Goober and got into the lounge.

So Goober and I searched away the afternoon. In order to get my two dollars worth, we must have parked forty or fifty times. We covered the whole island at least once and parts of it two or three times.

And we found not one single lousy alligator.

We finally gave up, retrieved the sissy members of our family, and went home. As we left the island, the purveyor of alligator maps gave us a nice smile and big wave. My wife waved back. I ignored him. Goober stuck his tongue out at him.

19. SAINT SIMONS SINNERS

After having observed the dexterity exhibited by senior bicyclists on St. Simons and Jekyll Islands, Yankees and Southerners alike, I have come to the conclusion it is time to organize a Senior Citizen Motorcycle Club. Such an organization will not only bring happy benefits to its members, it will also generate notoriety for the Golden Isles. There will be obstacles, but I am confident we can overcome them.

We will need a brief period of transition training, since I understand driving one of those powerful "hogs" is slightly different from riding a bicycle, and we will need a practice area which can be sealed off from the prying eyes of the general public. The new Sea Island Golf Course comes to mind as a likely site. The grass growing along the golf cart trails will cushion the fall of those who have trouble balancing, and the authorities there are skilled at sealing off areas from the prying eyes of the general public.

We will obtain some surplus army steel helmets and paint them black to match our leather jackets. The club name and logo should reflect our base of operation and be sufficiently intimidating to assure the respect of other bikers. I suggest as an emblem a savage porpoise in the act of eating a swimmer, and for a name, I propose SAINT SIMONS SINNERS.

It will abbreviate into the intimidating anagram "SSS," which can be painted as triple lightning bolts.

I anticipate some members will try to ride in side cars rather than astride a powerful two wheeler. But on this matter we stand firm. Side cars will be strictly reserved for club members who pass their ninetieth birthday and visiting grandchildren too large to fit into the small-child handlebar seats. There will be no coddling in the "SSS."

Once organized, we will send out good will squadrons to visit other cities, but our main area of operations will be St. Simons Island. Each Saturday night we will gather to ride around the island four abreast, weaving in and out in daring patterns and rearing back to do breathtaking "wheelies" as we activate our manifold cutoffs and emit roaring VROOOOMS!

Following our thrilling display, we will assemble at Neptune Park to drink beer and answer questions of admiring fans who, I anticipate, will gather around in great number. It is likely a number of local policemen will also gather around to ask questions. We will refer these to our Public Relations and Police Liaison Committee, which will be composed of retired judges, former police chiefs, and a number of lawyers.

Now that I have identified, and solved, all potential problems, I am ready to accept applications for membership. All I have left to do is announce the project to my wife, who does not yet know about it.

On second thought, hold up on those applications. I will get back to you.

20. STONEWALL

Jo-Jack Johnson is probably the best dog trainer in all Georgia. Not only are his dogs good hunters, they are known for other smarts too, like biting strangers, fetching, and riding in the back of pickup trucks without falling out.

There is not a single fire hydrant in the county where Jo-Jack lives, but his dogs do not seem to mind. All the male dogs easily learned to substitute trees for hydrants, but there was one exception. A big-raw boned hound named Stonewall learned to substitute Yankees.

No one seems to know exactly why or how Jo-Jack managed to teach him to do this, although the "why" can probably be traced to Jo-Jack's one visit to New York City.

Right next to Jo-Jack's property, his cousin, Big Booger Benson, has a makeshift Civil War souvenir shop. For passing motorists who cannot read the big blue and gray sign, there is a pair of wooden statues of Generals Ulysses S. Grant and Robert E. Lee standing on the front stoop.

Stonewall spent most of each day sleeping out in Jo-Jack's front yard, but whenever he heard a car stop at Big Booger's, he would open one eye and check the license plate. If it was from a Yankee state, he would lope over and greet its occupants as they got out of the car. Nine times out of ten, they got right back in and drove off. Then at the end of the day, Stonewall would amble over and deliver anything he had left over onto the statue of General Grant.

There was usually a lot left over, because not all that many Yankees stopped at the museum. Indeed, it is doubtful if more than half a dozen Yankees had ever been in the county at one time since 1864. Since Yankees were not critical to his business, Big Booger enjoyed seeing them get sprayed by a good ole Southern hound dog, but he got tired of washing off General Grant. So one day he went to his cousin and told him the next dog he caught lifting his leg on his property would likely get a load of bird shot in his rear end. Jo-Jack said if that dog happened to be Stonewall, then cousin Big Booger would likely be picking shot out of his own rear end.

Here the matter rested until one day Big Booger wrapped some bare wires around General Grant's leg and hooked them into the electric power lines running into his house. The jolt catapulted Stonewall across the road and sent him screaming into the woods, where he remained for the next three days. When he returned, he was a different dog.

Stonewall will no longer go near a Yankee, and the mere appearance of a northern car is enough to send him yelping for cover. Jo-Jack spent weeks trying to rehabilitate his beloved Stonewall, but he finally gave up. He is now trying to train a replacement, but so far without success. It seems they broke the mold when they made Stonewall.

I tell you all this in case you should someday run across Big Booger's Civil War Museum and Souvenir Shop. It may be safe to stop, but you can't be sure. After all, Jo-Jack is probably the best dog trainer in all Georgia.

ˉ21. SOUTHERN DINNER GUESTS

Numerous Yankees have asked what Southerners prefer to eat. The information was sought mostly by Yankees seeking to repay social debts. I am happy to be able to provide this information.

Contrary to what you might think, Southerners enjoy the same food that appeals to Yankees. Preparing a dinner party for Southern guests need not be all that different from what you are used to doing. However, for a special treat for special Southern friends, serve hog jowls.

You may have to go beyond your common, run-of-the-mill super-market to find hog jowls, but the search is worth it. Few other meats provide the nutritional value for the price.

For an accompanying dish, serve grits. Unlike Yankees, who tend to eat grits only with breakfast -- if at all -- Southerners eat grits at any meal. And remember, grits can be boiled or fried or baked or grilled and served hot or cold, or any old temperature you like.

Include either fried green tomatoes or butter beans on the menu. They will preclude your having to bother with a salad. Pecan pie is a must for dessert.

One of the nice things about gracious Southern dining is the absence of a cluttered array of different drinks. Only one is necessary to entertain Southerners. It is the locally brewed Georgia liquor known by various names: white lightning, hooch, back-woods booze, Georgia rhapsody, etc. Whatever the name, you can tell if it's the real McCoy by the absence of any type of government seal.

Georgia rhapsody may be offered before, during, and after dinner. It is usually served in empty mayonnaise jars, but for a touch of elegance, use cocktail glasses before dinner and wine glasses during the meal. After dinner, liquor glasses are proper, or if you pass around cigars, brandy snifters.

I know many of you are wondering if substitutions are possible. The answer is yes. According to the season and availability, possum can be substituted for hog jowls, but remember, possum cannot be eaten in the months containing the letter "i". Store-bought bourbon can be served instead of Georgia rhapsody. But if it is, don't forget to gather a supply of branch water for mixers.

Contrary to popular Yankee misconception, Southerners use knives, forks, and spoons, just like Yankees do. In fact, Southern hostesses will tell you Southerners were eating with proper utensils when Yankees were still spearing meat with hunting knives. Indeed, Southerners are said to lay out place settings with no less than fifteen different silver utensils artfully clustered around the plate.

I am not sure that this is true, but just to be on the safe side, put out all the silverware you have and then lie. Say the table is just too small to hold the rest of your silver. If you serve enough Georgia rhapsody no one is going to care anyway.

22. TOUR SHIP WELCOME

I, for one, miss the tour ships which used to dock at the foot of Mallory Street on their excursions up and down the inland waterway. I suspect the Village merchants do too.

On behalf of these merchants and the many citizens of St. Simons who marveled at the majesty of these ships, I propose the Chamber of Commerce organize a gala island welcome to entice the excursion line to once more direct its ships to the village fishing pier. In furtherance of this worthwhile project, I submit the following modest plan:

The arriving ship will be met by a crowd of Georgians paddling dugout canoes, shouting hospitable greetings, and blowing kisses to the lady passengers. They will be clad in traditional Georgia dress -- baseball hats, muscle shirts, and faded overalls. Next will come lines of shrimp boats and small pleasure cruisers, blowing whistles and squirting plumes of water in the air from garden hoses.

As the ship docks, the canoe paddlers will dive for coins thrown from the deck, and passengers will be serenaded by the Good Ole Boys' Honkey Tonk Ensemble and a local high school marching band playing Dixie and Sweet Georgia Brown. Strolling along the pier carrying colorful parasols will be a dozen lovely Georgia belles dressed as Scarlett O'Hara. Escorting them will be a like number of Rhett's, doffing their top hats and flashing Clark Gable smiles. All of them will be available on the pier to have their pictures taken with the visitors when they land.

After suitable welcoming speeches by local politicians -- local politicians are always ready to deliver welcoming speeches -- the passengers will disembark under a large banner reading: "WELCOME YANKEES. WE LOVE YOU."

Southerners may consider such a banner a bit "too much," but they should realize most of those passengers will be Yankees, and Yankees tend to spend a lot more money in places where they feel loved. The monetary return to be gleaned far outweighs the twinges of conscience to be suffered.

Once on the pier, passengers will find an assortment of

food booths selling traditional Southern favorites: grits, possum nuggets, collard greens, etc. There will also be a booth selling Northern "haute" cuisine: hotdogs, bagels, and hamburgers.

The ship departure will be as colorful and memorable as the arrival, with everything running in reverse.

Admittedly, there will be a certain expense connected with all this, but I am confident the bills can be met. Surely Village merchants will kick in a share of their lucrative profits, and the cruise line should add a substantial amount from the two or three hundred buck surcharge passengers will gladly pay to experience a St. Simons Welcome. Those who do not wish to pay the surcharge can be locked in the hold while the ship is in port.

Finally, there will also be all the money retrieved by those coin divers.

23. SOUTHERN FEET

It has long been recognized that, on average, Southerners are better swimmers than Yankees, and the margin of superiority increases inversely with the latitude. It was long thought this phenomenon was a function of the weather: a longer swimming season translated into more experienced swimmers. But recent discoveries have shown that weather has nothing to do with it. It is a question of feet.

Feeding data gathered over twenty years into a high speed computer, the American Footwear Manufacturers Association (AFMA) discovered Southern feet are slightly flattened from lack of shoe restraint during the formative years. Of course some Yankee children go barefoot too, but not for as long as their Southern counterparts, simply because snow clogs up between toes and makes walking difficult.

The early expansion of Southern feet gives the Southerner a distinct edge over the Yankee in swimming and other activities involving the lower extremities, such as bug stomping and ballet dancing. The ballet advantage is not due so much to the widened feet, but to the super strong toes that come with going barefoot. Whenever you see a ballerina stomping around the stage entirely on her tippytoes, you can bet she is from the Deep South.

This toe development associated with going barefoot also explains why Southerners have prehensile toes. Not many Yankees realize this. As Southerners reach their early thirties and learn to wear shoes, there is little occasion for the offhand acquaintance or casual bystander to observe the dexterity of the Southern toe. But in case you doubt these Southern toes are prehensile, just watch the way a Southern beachgoer picks up sea shells.

Because of the innate advantage Southerners enjoy by virtue of their feet, there are Yankees who seek to obtain offsetting compensation in contests and endeavors which involve the feet. I think this is ridiculous and feel I speak for the majority of Yankees who, by and large, completely reject the idea. I say live and let live and let the feet fall where they may.

48

I bring the foregoing to the attention of all you Yankee readers, not for you to seek parity with Southern competitors, but so you can prudently observe certain rules while down South:

1) Do not bet on Yankee swimmers racing against Southerners.
2) If you feel an urge to be a ballet dancer, join a troupe up North where everyone will be falling off their toes just like you are.
3) Above all, never get into a bug-stomping contest with a Southerner.

24. SEA ISLAND ATTRACTIONS

I would like to dispel a vicious rumor that has discouraged many Yankees from viewing one of the area's most impressive sights. The rumor has it that only Jaguar and Ferrari automobiles are allowed on Sea Island.

This is not so. Mercedes-Benzes, Lincolns, Cadillacs, and Chryslers are also found there. As a matter of fact, other makes of cars are also allowed as long as they are clean, not too old, and gone by nightfall. I know this for a fact, for my wife and I frequently drive through Sea Island, and we have not once been stopped -- followed, perhaps, but not stopped.

This should come as a welcomed revelation to all Yankees in the area, because Sea Island homes are among the most beautiful you will find anywhere in the world. What makes them particularly special is the landscaping. It is immaculate, and when you combine live oak trees with immaculate landscaping, you really have a treat to behold.

My wife and I used to visit Sea Island more often than we do now, because of a particular lot which was for sale. It was right there on a corner of the main street, and in the middle of it was a great sign which said, "FOR SALE, 650,000 DOLLARS."

We were enthralled. Both of us consider anything over ten thousand dollars strictly in the realm of big government. My wife delighted in caressing the sign and getting her picture taken beside it. One day we talked a friend of ours into donning her real estate sales jacket and getting her picture taken shaking hands with my wife standing beside the sign. In her hand she held a "Sold" sign. We take a copy of the photo with us when we visit our Yankee friends up North. It impresses them.

You can imagine our disappointment when we drove by one day and found the sign had been taken down. Rumor has it that a rich trial lawyer has purchased the lot and is having a special house, one that would befit the location, transported in from overseas. Supposedly it is coming from India where a huge work force is being trained for the considerable task of dismantling the building, brick by brick, for shipping.

Frankly, I doubt very much if there is anything to this rumor. Yet you never know.

If any of you readers have a hankering to someday see the Taj Mahal in its original setting, I suggest you go now.

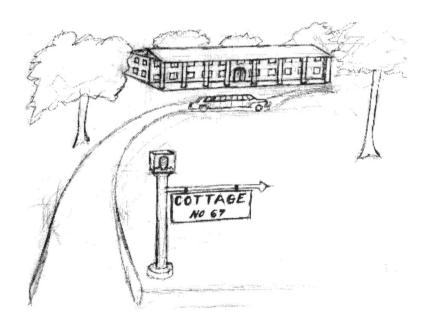

25. SOUTHERN CONCEPTION

On behalf of a Southern friend of mine, I would like to announce the upcoming appearance of the fabulous "Braxton Bragg Beautiful Baby Boutique, a Sperm Bank for Southern Ladies of Quality Who Care." I normally refuse to take part in the promotion of commercial enterprises, particularly ones with long names, but in this case I make an exception. I do so partially because of my friendship with Braxton Bragg and partially because I think his campaign to protect Southern grandfathers could also protect Yankees. Let me explain.

It all began a few months ago when Braxton's daughter, Betty Boo, announced she was going to have a baby. You would think such an announcement would have thrilled Braxton, particularly since Betty Boo is his only child; but instead, it provoked a violent outburst. You see, there was a complication: Betty Boo is a successful businesswoman who has accumulated just about everything possible except a husband. Nor is she interested in obtaining one. But she does want a child, and with her biological clock loudly ticking away the years, she turned to a do-it-yourself outfit known as a sperm bank.

Braxton had always dreamed of having a son-in-law he could terrorize and boss around, so he was not too happy over being a test tube grandfather. There wasn't much he could do about it, however. He sat around and sulked for a while and then decided to visit Betty Boo and take a look at the closest thing to a son-in-law he was ever going to get. He was shocked at what he found.

Expecting to at least see a picture of his future grandchild's father, he was dismayed to find the sperm donors were only identified by IQ, age, and general characteristics. Then it dawned on Braxton that since Betty Boo and the sperm bank were located in a large city close to the Mason Dixon Line, his grandchild might very well turn out to be a Yankee, or at least half Yankee. He visualized the raised eyebrows of his friends back in Georgia when he showed off his grandson and the kid started talking like a New

Yorker. The vision was so horrible, Braxton took to his bed with a severe headache which lasted three days.

But Braxton is a fighter, and at the end of three days, he came up swinging. He investigated the feasibility of abortion, adoption, and legal action, and finally decided to drive the sperm banks operating in the South out of business through competition. The Braxton Bragg Beautiful Baby etc. is to be the first of a series of new modern sperm banks which will eventually blanket the South.

The reception room will be painted a restful Confederate gray, and the strains of Dixie will be softly played over the internal sound system. Prospective mothers and their fathers will be received by pleasant, knowledgeable hostesses who will take them to private viewing rooms for a slide presentations of potential fathers. If requested, selected candidates will be available for interview by the soon-to-be grandfathers.

All vital statistics of the donors will be available. These will not only include IQ, age, characteristics, and place of birth, but also ancestry back to at least 1860. The fees charged will vary, depending on the donor's pedigree. Thus, the sperm from a descendant of a Georgia Civil War general would carry a higher price than that of an individual whose great, great, great grandfather was a Kentucky colonel. The prices would be graduated downward to a Confederate private of infantry, whose descendant's sperm could be had at a bargain basement price

When Braxton first approached me to help promote his chain of sperm banks, I turned him down, since Yankees do not normally worry about such things. But then I got to thinking there might be some Yankee women who could be adversely affected by that border city sperm bank. My Boston friend Kevin O'Mally would blow his Irish stack if one of his grandkids talked like a Southerner, and my buddy, Brooklyne Babe Costiliano would probably disown his daughter if she had a child with a drawl.

In view of all this, I finally agreed to help Braxton, but only if he would add an annex to his sperm bank for use by

Yankee women who happened to be down south and wanted a Yankee sire for their offspring. The annex would be painted blue and a separate sound system would play the Battle Hymn of the Republic. Sperm donors would all be Yankees and, in keeping with democratic principles, all prices would be the same -- cheap.

Braxton, who could not understand why any woman would want a Yankee baby, resisted the idea. However, he finally agreed to put a Yankee annex in the basement when I added one more concession: I agreed to turn down any future requests from existing sperm banks to participate in their donor programs.

Actually, this was not that much of a concession. Just between you and me, I have yet to be asked to participate in a sperm donor program. Of course, I have not yet checked today's mail.

26. SNAKE HANDLING

Earlier I provided Yankees a ste- by-step guide to recognizing a pit viper and identifying it as either a water moccasin, rattlesnake, or copperhead. The identification involved grasping the snake firmly by the neck and holding its head approximately a foot away at eye level. You may recall, a question arose as to how one went about accomplishing the grasping.

I am happy to report, after making another trip to Bubba Burke's Reptile Farm and Scientific Research Center, I now have the answer. The short answer is, "very carefully." The long answer is also, "very carefully," but there is more to it than that.

Bubba says he uses a long stick with a fork at the end, and I suggest you do the same. The idea is to place the fork of the stick around the base of the snake's head and pin it to the ground. You then keep pressure on the stick with your left hand and grasp the snake firmly with your right hand, assuming you are right handed, just behind the fork.

Bubba emphasized the adverb "firmly." He also pointed out it was important the fork catch the snake well up close to the head, because that head is where the fangs are located, and we do not want those fangs flopping around in the air when we reach down to grasp the neck.

Now, as you grasp the snake just behind the head with your right hand, drop the stick and immediately latch on to him about two thirds of the way down his body with your left hand. This is important. If that body is unrestrained, you are likely to find it wrapped tightly around your right arm. If this should happen, do not panic. Just retain a firm grasp on the neck and get a companion to unwrap the coils of the snake while you hold the head, and fangs, at arm's length. Admittedly there is a catch to this last procedure. If your companion happens to be another Yankee, the chances are he will be well on his way out of the area just when you need him.

The best way to handle this situation is to avoid it. Just

get both hands on that snake at the beginning like you are supposed to. Bubba suggests practicing with a length of thick rope before venturing out in the woods.

Finally we come to the proper release of the snake, once you have identified it as a pit viper. This part is simple. Just throw the thing as far away as possible and run like mad in the opposite direction. Bubba says this does not require practice. Both the throwing and the running are built-in instinctive reactions controlled entirely by the nervous system.

Now you know everything the average Yankee will ever need to know about snakes.

Good luck.

27. KINGS BAY

Sometime ago I visited Kings Bay to check out its suitability as a site for Yankees to visit. Here I ran into as tight a security system as I have ever seen.

After producing eight documents of identification and leaving my wife at the gate for security, I was admitted into the administrative portion of the base. Housing, recreational facilities, snack bars, and clubs were all neatly clustered along clean streets. It was all very impressive, but when I tried to reach the dock area, I was barred by towering fences and armed guards. Even though I crossed my heart and promised not to tell anyone what I saw, they still refused to let me proceed.

I finally gave up, reclaimed my wife, and left. I was disappointed, but happy over the diligence with which my Armed Forces guarded military secrets. I reasoned that if entry was denied anyone as nonthreatening and tightlipped as I am, then no enemy agent stood a chance of penetrating the security area.

With this as a background, I was dismayed to pick up the paper a while later and see a picture of a Russian colonel, followed by a drove of reporters, touring the docks of Kings Bay Submarine Base. You can imagine my shock.

Not only are newspaper reporters the biggest blabbermouths in all the world, that Russian colonel works for the only country with the means and desire to destroy the Tritdent delivery system. The caption under the picture said he was merely a member of a disarmament committee. Sure he was! My guess is he ran right back to the Kremlin and yakked his head off about everything he had seen.

As disturbing as all this was, I was convinced there was a logical explanation. As everyone knows, our Armed Forces do nothing that is illogical. I put my mind to figuring it out and believe I have found the answer.

The Kings Bay Submarine base is a gigantic sham.

The way I see it, the whole thing is a clever bluff to thwart the evil forces of the world. The only thing the base contains is an incomplete giant submarine hulk. It sits there at the pier to impress selected visitors and is towed out to sea periodically to offer photo opportunities. Its name is changed frequently to support the contention that there is a whole fleet of submarines, and a bunch of sailors sit around snack bars with uniforms bearing the names of imaginary boats.

Tridident missile mock-ups are built into the unfinished hull. With enough prior notice, the Navy can organize carefully orchestrated guided tours which leave visitors with the desired impression. Even Congress participates in the elaborate subterfuge by appropriating adequate funds to procure and support the hypothetical Trident fleet.

Now that I have figured out the situation, I feel much better, and also much safer. I hope you do too.

My next project is to determine what the Navy has done with all that money Congress has appropriated.

28. GRANDPARENT FOLLIES

On mornings of days surrounding holidays, such as the day after Thanksgiving and the day before Easter, grandparents appear in force at the Neptune Park playground. While their visiting offspring sleep in, grandma and grandpa take their grandchildren to the park to show them off and let them play on the slides and swings and monkey bars.

These grandparent follies are very colorful affairs. Children and grandparents frolic among the equipment, bouncing off one another, teetering, dodging, and getting sand in their shoes. Not all the grandparents participate, however. Many of them just sit on the benches wearing smug expressions befitting grandparents of superior children.

Participating grandparents normally fall into two groups: those with very small toddlers, and those whose grandchildren are being brought up according to rules dictated by the new progressive child-rearing experts. In other words, brats.

The brat handlers and toddler tenders are joined in the arena only occasionally by grandparent spectators whose grandchildren have fallen off swings or wet their pants and by stupid grandfathers. It was in this latter capacity that I joined my granddaughter Pruney at the slide.

Pruney was a tiny little thing at the time, barely three years old and a bit shy. I talked her into climbing up to the top of the slide, but there she froze, effectively blocking all the other kids who wanted to slide.

Unable to reach her from where I stood, I had no choice but to climb up the slide ladder to fetch her. Once on top, I found myself hemmed in by kids who had followed me up. There was nowhere to go but down that slide, so I took Pruney on my lap and pushed off. It seemed like a good idea at the time.

We traveled maybe three feet and stuck fast. Those stupid, short sighted slide designers had produced a slide that only accommodated narrow beamed kids, without regard for more fully formed grandfathers. It was all very embarrassing. The other grandparents fixed me with accusing stares, and I knew they were thinking unkind thoughts about old men in their second childhood.

After a few unsuccessful jiggles, I raised part of my posterior onto the edge of the slide. ZIP! We went shooting down that slide and came to rest in a dignity-shattering welter of sand. The raised edges of that slide were designed to keep little kids inside and to carve deep grooves into anything riding along their tops.

Pruney was delighted with the ride and wanted to do it again, but I talked her into joining me for an ice cream cone instead. We ate standing up, a position I favored for several days thereafter.

Since that day, playground activity has been strictly a spectator sport as far as I am concerned. I recommend it as such to all grandparents, Yankees and Southerners alike.

29. ELECTRONIC ENHANCEMENT

I do not suppose most of you have given much thought to electronic enhancement of musical instruments. I had not done so myself until I ran into a young Yankee inventor named Yako Henderson, who is also a short order cook and a member of a local rock band known as the Grungies.

Yako looks more like a grungie than an inventor, but he is an electronic genius who hooks wires onto vibrating strings of musical instruments, thereby increasing their volume by at least nine hundred percent. He is now working on a method of electronically enhancing trumpets.

This is difficult to do, because the vibrations emanating from trumpets come from the vibrating lips of the trumpet players. It is hard to find trumpet players willing to have their lips wired, even for the sake of science. This is because trumpet players are vain and do not like to walk around with wires hanging off their lips.

Nevertheless, Yako is making progress. He explains that eventually the wires will run up past the sinuses and out an ear to a barely visible plug. The wires will hardly be noticeable at all until plugged into external electronic enhancement equipment. Properly wired and adjusted, a trumpeter with the Southwest Secondary School Marching Band will sound just like Harry James. And here is the exciting part: Yako points out that if lips can be wired, so can vocal cords. The music world stands on the brink of revolution.

Imagine the excitement that will be generated when Perry Como's vocal cords are electronically restored to their vibratory excellence of yesteryear. And how the world will applaud when Frank Sinatra sounds the same as he did in his youth. Droves of Frankie admirers will throw away their walkers and come screaming out of retirement to don bobby socks and swoon over their idol as they did in the late '40's.

Of course there may be a problem matching aging bodies with rejuvenated vocal cords, but I figure an electric jolt or two to the nervous system will do the trick. I once witnessed the therapeutic effect of electricity when my Uncle

Charley tried to repair our electric toaster. At seventy years old, Charley performed a graceful triple backward somersault out the kitchen door and over the dining room table. He could not have done that when he was twenty.

Yako points out there is still much to be done before the electronic enhancement is ready for full scale testing. He hopes to try it out locally first, in about two years, hopefully using The Good Old Boys Honkey-Tonk-Dixieland Ensemble as the test vehicle.

So, if you happen to be watching the Good Old Boys when the leader suddenly goes skittering across the dance floor belting out Sweet Georgia Brown loud enough to shake the rafters, you will know young Yankee Yako is about to become a millionaire.

30. EPHRAM BUBBA

From time to time I get an urge to do something daring. The feeling goes away as fast as it arrives, however, and I never get the same urge twice -- except in the case of the St. Simons toll booth.

Every time I get to that toll booth a small voice whispers, "Go ahead, run on through without paying." So far I have been able to fight off the urge, primarily because of the rumored dire consequences of such an act. I have heard that the running of a toll booth red light sets off alarms in every law enforcement office in Georgia. SWAT teams as far away as Atlanta are alerted, horns sound, sirens blare, and highway patrolmen converge from all directions.

Consequences are particularly tough for Yankees. I understand Georgia has a special prison just for them in Andersonville. The stories told about the Yankee prison in Andersonville make Alcatraz and Sing Sing sound like vacation resorts.

This is why I have gone to great pains to remain law abiding since arriving in Georgia, and I advise all other Yankees to do the same. It does not pay to fool with Georgia gendarmes. Take my cousin Ephram, for example.

Ephram was a chronic speeder, and when he moved to Georgia, he picked up two speeding tickets in rapid succession. The arresting officers were very large Georgians who did not take kindly to Yankee speeders, and neither did the Southern judges who laid heavy fines upon Ephram.

As a two time loser, Ephram realized he would have to make a real effort to avoid future arrests. And he did.

He went to night school to learn to speak Southern, traded his car in for a pick up truck, bought a Labrador retriever named Beauregard to ride in the back, painted Confederate flags on the sides, and covered the tail gate with bumper stickers. One of them said "Yankee Go Home!," another suggested women drivers be banned from the road, and a third called for three cheers for Robert E. Lee. He changed his middle name to "Bubba" and got a new driver's license. When he was finally ready, he invited me to go along with him for a test spin. With Beauregard howling in the back, we went barreling down I-95 like a runaway rocket.

It was not long before we were pulled over by a Georgia State Police car. Beaming with confidence, Ephram exercised his jaw muscles preparatory to speaking Southern as we waited for the law man to get out and approach us. When at last he did, he wasn't a "he" at all, but a "she," and a petit little "she" at that.

Ephram was taken back when she appeared, but he recovered rapidly and said, with a big smile, "Where y'all from, Honeychile?"

She took out her pad, looked him right in the eye, and said, "Cincinnati. May I see your license, please?"

I buy a batch of cookies every week. Beauregard and I eat some of them and we send the rest to Ephram in Andersonville. I don't know whether he gets them or not, but it is the least we can do.

31. JEKYLL ISLAND PARKING FEE

One of the most ingenious methods of raising money I know of is the Jekyll Island parking fee which every visitor is required to pay as he arrives on the island.

One might be inclined to grouse over paying a toll to drive over a causeway such as the one leading to Jekyll, particularly if he has to wait for a drawbridge, but who would begrudge the islanders a couple of bucks worth of parking fees? Besides, a free strip map comes with the deal, along with a pleasant greeting from the parking attendant.

New York Yankees are particularly impressed. Not only do they have to pay a hefty bridge or tunnel fee to get on the island of Manhattan, once there they pay through the nose for the privilege of parking. And those toll takers are anything but pleasant.

I know of a New Yorker who spent the better part of a month vacationing on St. Simons. Every day he drove to Jekyll Island just to take advantage of the good deal offered by way of the two dollar parking fee. He spent all day long moving from one parking spot to another and on a good day might park in forty different locations. This averaged out at a paltry five cents a park. In New York it would have cost him maybe fifty bucks for one park, and his car would probably have been vandalized to boot.

I could never understand why other Georgia communities did not learn from the Jekyll experience and develop a similar system of their own. Darien, for example, might block all incoming roads except Route 17 and charge out of state cars a few bucks for the privilege of parking in the community. This would enable the town to honor its heritage by erecting a statue of a Highlander. Such a statue would also provide visitors an excuse to stop.

Other locations might benefit, but the most obvious place to install a Jekyll type system is on the causeway leading to St. Simons Island. Since St. Simons is at least three times the size of Jekyll, with correspondingly more places to park, a six dollar fee would be appropriate. Even if inhabitants of the island were exempt, the enhanced parking fee should more than cover the revenue currently collected as causeway tolls.

The only reason I can think of that this has not been done is because authorities do not know where to spend all that extra money. If so, I think I may be able to help.

32. FREDERICA

Yankees arriving in the Golden Isles should visit Fort Frederica on St. Simons Island. As one of the cradles of colonial Georgia, it provides a glimpse into the soul of the 13th Colony and lays the foundation for understanding the way things were, are, and will be here in Coastal Georgia.

The site of Frederica is now a national park, complete with visitors center, movie theater, and a set of well-groomed, friendly rangers brimming with congeniality. In fact, the whole place is congenial. There is even a sign as you leave which says, "Thank you for visiting your park." I think this is a nice touch, but I warn you, it will cost you two dollars to visit your park.

Actually not everyone has to pay two dollars. Certain groups, such as those in drug rehabilitation centers, get in free. And those over 62 can buy a golden age passport for ten bucks and visit the park for nothing.

This golden age passport is most worthwhile, and I urge all Yankees of sufficient age to get one. Not only does it get you into national parks all over the country, everyone with you gets in free too. Thus, you can round up all the kids and grandkids, cram them into a station wagon, and take the whole crew to a national park without paying a penny. In fact, your guests do not even have to be members of your family. Even nodding acquaintances qualify.

This apparent oversight by the National Park Service has opened up an interesting loophole through which at least one enterprising Yankee has crawled. He is a retired something or other who breaks the monotony of basking in the Georgia sun by taking tourists on cut-rate tours of Frederica National Monument.

Known locally as Old Sam, or Uncle Sam, he has a valid ten dollar golden age passport and will take as many people as will fit into a car on a tour of Frederica for a dollar a head, fifty cents for veterans. This is not a bad deal at all, particularly if you are a veteran. You may not rate the privileges of a drug rehabilitation enrollee, but Sam will save you a buck and a half.

Now, you might think what Sam is doing is illegal, but this is not so. The rangers at Frederica are well aware of Sam's activities, for the rangers at Frederica are very smart people. But because of the nature of their organization, they are also bureaucrats.

Bureaucrats learn early on that rules are rules, and regulations are regulations, and the best way to get along is to follow them and not make waves. Making waves may be defined as calling attention to loopholes in instructions put out by the front office. If that front office happens to be in Washington D.C., the risk is even greater, because government workers in Washington simply do not make mistakes.

So, Old Sam is likely to be in business for a long, long time. As a veteran, I wish him well.

33. BOYS AND GIRLS

Today we divert from our normal format to discuss various ways of telling boys from girls, men from women, males from females. Just a few short decades ago, such a discussion would have been ridiculous, akin to discussing how to recognize up from down. But that was then and this is now.

Back in my day, the two sexes were easy to tell apart: females wore skirts and males wore trousers; girls had long hair, boys did not. Other than for finger adornment, the only ones who wore rings were women, pirates, and bulls -- and bulls wore them in the nose. Men had muscles, smoked cigars, and sometimes swore. Women did not.

All that has changed, as you know. Men now sport coffers hanging down to their shoulders and chins, while women vie to see who can sport the shortest butch cut, or shiniest bald head. Earrings and necklaces are as likely to adorn male ears and necks as they are to appear on ladies.

Not long ago I heard a young woman driver deliver to a fellow motorist a stream of unflattering adjectives I had never heard before, complete with gestures that would have shamed a Roman taxi driver. She was GOOD! And I knew she was a woman because she was nursing a baby when she drove by me. As for biceps , I recently visited the hospital to see my friend Larry. He had said "sir" to the bouncer/bartender at a local bar, only to discover the hard way that "sir" was a "ma'am," and a mighty muscular ma'am at that.

I mention all this, not in the way of criticism, since I am a great admirer of the "now generation," or whatever the current crop of youth is calling itself. Rather I seek to assist in the growing problem of how to tell the sexes apart. Nor is it only my generation who faces this difficulty. I have noticed that many of the young men who wear earrings and long hair, also wear beards. I can only conclude they do so because they are tired of being mistaken for females by their peers. Therefore, in passing on these tips as to how to tell men from women, I address all generations.

Tip 1. Obviously the wearing of a beard or mustache is a sure giveaway that the individual is a male, although one can never be sure but what some lady inventor will eventually come up with a way for women to grow them. Besides, not all men wear beards, so Tip 1 has its limitations.

Tip 2. If you are a male on a crowded bus and a doubtful individual gets on, get up and offer your seat. If the newcomer takes it, he is a man. A modern woman will stand and sneer at you.

Tip 3. If there are several doubtfulls in a group, shout, "Well, as I live and breath here comes Lenora Babbitt," and note the reaction. Women will look toward the entrance and smile a greeting. The men will shudder and leave by the other door.

Tip 4. Carry a small tape recorder playing a recording of Bella Abzug singing I AM WOMAN! Both men and women will snap to attention, but only women will give the clinched fist salute.

Tip 5. Stand by the public bathroom until the doubtful person uses it. Normally the men will go to the door marked "men" and the women to the ladies' side. But don't count on it, particularly in an area where school officials embrace the new modern system of teaching reading.

Tip 6. Smell the individual. Women are inclined to wear perfume, while men lean toward after-shave lotion. However, it is becoming ever more difficult to tell the difference as the two come closer together in fragrance. Besides, young men and women of today are turning increasingly to the universal uni-odor called "perspiration."

Tip 7. Avoid referring to strangers as "he" or "she," and avoid calling anyone a gender specific name, such as "ma'am" or "sir." This final tip will not aid you in differentiating between male and female, but it will keep you out of trouble and avoid hospital bills. Just ask my friend Larry.

34. YANKEE PRE-SCHOOL

I have heard Yankees complain about political discrimination practiced by local government officials in this part of Georgia. This is all hogwash. I have been treated kindly by all Southern officials -- with the possible exception of the traffic policeman whose pants leg got caught in my bicycle chain.

To these Yankee critics of local officialdom, I have nothing but scorn. To quash their complaints, I ask, "Just where else will you find a Southern county providing free head-start training to little Yankee children? "

Now, admittedly, this program has not yet been offered, but I understand it is under active consideration. I received this inside information by way of a brother of my friend's mother-in-law's second cousin, who just happens to be in a position to know.

The requirement for such pre-school training was first brought to light by first grade teachers who noticed their little Yankee pupils were scoring two full letter grades below their classmates. A follow-up government study confirmed this and uncovered the cause: the Yankee kids simply did not understand their teachers.

Needless to say, this situation not only inhibits learning, it makes it difficult for teachers to establish discipline in the classroom. One harassed schoolmarm summed it up as follows: "When I say, 'Yallgit,' I want them Yankee kids to git, right along with the rest of them young'uns."

The proposed special classes would alleviate the problem by teaching little pre-school Yankees to understand the melodic flow of Georgia speech, thereby enabling them to enter first grade on an equal footing with their classmates.

Of course there are always detractors. There are those who think Yankee parents should foot the bill for this training, arguing that they were the ones who taught their kids to speak Yankee in the first place. To these cold-hearted reactionaries we say, "How about all those poor Yankees who cannot afford such training? Is there not a danger they will seek the services of some cut-rate quack who does more harm than good?"

A case in point is a certain poor Yankee family living on Sea Island. Unable to afford a proper tutor, they turned over the task of coaching their little daughter to a servant from Tide-water Virginia. On her first day of school the poor little girl got her "oots" and "aboots" all mixed up with Georgia Southern and Yankee. It was such a traumatic experience, she now resists all efforts to teach her anything at all.

I am sure all you readers will back the Yankee pre-school program and work to see it come about. If you run into anyone who opposes the idea, just tell him the story of that poor little Sea Island girl. And if that doesn't work, look him right in the eye and say, "Yallgit!"

35. CATFISH

I have often heard Yankees remark on the speed at which Southerners are able to eat catfish. No Yankee can touch them. In fact, the average Southerner will devour four catfish, leaving only the bones, while a Yankee is still working his way through his first one.

Until recently it was thought this ability was derived from experience alone, but now science has provided a superior explanation. It is a question of teeth.

Over the years Southern teeth have evolved to contain minute grooves on the back side which neatly and rapidly separate the catfish meat from the bones. Activated by a suction created in the throat, these grooves, vibrating several hundred times a minute, allow the eater to pass the catfish from left to right across his mouth in a continuous motion. Bones drop below onto the plate, or ground, while the flesh is retained in the mouth for processing.

Yankees, who do not have grooved teeth, must resort to the old, and slow, conventional method of picking out the catfish bones. However, I am happy to report dental science has discovered a way to help Yankee catfish lovers. A simple procedure, completed in half a day, turns Yankee dentures into Southern catfish chompers so perfect only a licensed dentist can tell the difference between the two.

The procedure was perfected by Archibald Fobbledoner, a dental assistant from a little town not far from Waycross. While awaiting certification by the Association of American Dentists, he is forced to work out of a shed behind his house, but he comes highly recommended by the Catfish Chefs of Southern Georgia.

Unfortunately, there is one drawback to the procedure. It is expensive. Fobbledoner gets about $500 for the work, give or take twenty dollars or so depending on the number of teeth the patient has left. However, if you are fortunate enough to have false teeth, you can have them done for perhaps half that price. Fobbledoner has constructed an ingenious machine that clamps onto a set of dentures and rotates them 360 degrees as it grinds out the grooves in one continuous motion. The machine will also work on regular teeth, but it is hard on the patient's neck. Besides, most people are adverse to being rotated around their teeth.

There is also a side benefit to the procedure. It involves kissing. As many people know, Southerners are great kissers. Apparently the skill is derived from those catfish-demolishing teeth, which begin vibrating in the heat of passion to drive Yankees wild. Yankee catfish eaters who have had the operation not only report a fourfold increase in their catfish-eating speed, but also a significant improvement in their love life.

I caution the reader I cannot vouch for this beneficial side effect, because I have not researched the matter personally as I had hoped to do. You see, my wife is from New Jersey, and she has informed me that if I want the matter researched, she will do the researching.

36. POSTAL PROGRESS

A Yankee friend of mine of the "once" generation recently complained of the cost and service of the United States Postal Service. He pointed out it cost three cents to send a letter when he was a boy, and now the same letter costs more than ten times as much. Also, he has to go out to the street to get his mail, whereas his parents only went as far as the front door.

I immediately jumped to the defense of our intrepid mail carriers, who continue to brave rain, snow, and gloom of night to keep us in touch with one another. What my friend and many others tend to overlook is all the postal progress that has been made over the same years. That 32 cent letter could cost a lot more, you know.

It is true that there has been a shift from the front door mail slot to curb-side mail boxes, but think of all the exercise mail receivers get, compared to their forefathers. The Post Office claims much of the credit for the increasing years of life expectancy enjoyed by Americans. The curb-side mailboxes also save mail deliverers time, shoe leather, and uniforms. Dogs find it very difficult to get inside a postal vehicle to bite the mail deliverer.

It is true that little saving was realized when curb-side boxes were first introduced. This was because mail carriers had to have long right arms to reach across the front seat and out the passenger side window to get to the mailbox. This limited the recruiting pool, and in response to market forces, a higher wage had to be paid to lure qualified candidates from other professions such as professional basketball playing. After a few years this handicap was overcome when an ingenious postal official thought of providing delivery vehicles with right hand drives. However, many of the old long-armed postal workers are still on the payroll. You can identify them by the elongated right arms which stretched, from years of reaching, to become several inches longer than the left ones.

The right hand drive vehicles allowed normal size people

to reach roadside mailboxes, but the savings were not immediately felt because only Japanese and English cars had right hand drives, and imported models were expensive. Finally, American "know how" came to the fore, and automobile manufacturers developed the ugly little white postal vehicles with right hand drives which are common today. These new automotive marvels also allowed American car manufacturers to enter the lucrative British and Japanese

markets. Perhaps you have seen them scurrying along the streets of Tokyo and London. Or perhaps not.

Another long stride in increasing the labor pool was made by the Post Office Department with the advent of the zip code. Before that important innovation, only those who could read at or above a sixth grade level could be hired for handling mail. All that has changed. In a few short hours, an illiterate individual can be taught to read numbers zero through nine -- providing he has all ten of his fingers. The five-digit zip code allows a much lower wage scale for mail sorters, and the addition of four more numbers to the code will eventually preclude the necessity for mail deliverers to read. All that remains to be done is to get the public to stop making sevens and ones look alike and to keep sixes and nines from appearing as zeros.

Here we hasten to assure our readers that none of the new wave of illiterate postal workers have yet been assigned to the St. Simons or Jekyll Island post offices. Every single one of our fine postal men and women can read and write, at least at the sixth grade level.

The Postal Service has always embraced the latest innovations of technology, be they right hand drive vehicles or jet airplanes. Back when my Yankee friend was a boy, it took six days for a first class letter to be carried by train from California to its East Coast destination. Now the same letter wings its way across country in a matter of a few hours. Of course, it still takes it six or seven days to be delivered, but at least that letter does not spend all that time in some smelly old railroad car. It now sits in a clean, neat, air conditioned post office among dedicated postal workers puzzling over sevens, ones, sixes, nines, and zeros.

Finally, as for that thirteen hundred percent increase in the price of a first class stamp, there are a lot of things which have increased ten fold in price over the same period. Take for example ....

Well, I cannot think of any right off hand this very minute, but surely there must be some.

37. TARIFFS

More than once have I heard Yankees complain about the higher prices charged for goods and services on St. Simons and Jekyll Islands than on the mainland. They were inclined to attribute the inflated price tags to entrepreneurial greed, but this is not so. The added costs are the result of the tariffs placed on all goods arriving from outside the islands.

Few people realize the purpose, or even the existence, of these tariffs. I am happy to be able to explain them as part of my ongoing educational services rendered to Yankees living in the Golden Isles.

The tariffs have been established to encourage the development of island industries with a view of making the islands self-sufficient by the year 2010. This will enable the islands to throw off the yoke of exploitation and proclaim their independence from Glynn County. "When in the course of human events, etc...."

If full independence is not feasible, at least the islands will be in position to negotiate a merger with a different county, preferably one with a lower tax base, or even another state. We are really not that far from either Florida or South Carolina, although a northern state is probably out of the question. Yankee governors have enough trouble keeping track of their own cities, and it can be argued that Florida has become Yankeefied enough to qualify if we really want to leave the South.

It has been suggested the tariff aids business owners but does so at the expense of labor and the common man. This is another misconception. The thirty-five cent toll charged mainland migrant workers provides the native St. Simons working man and woman an important advantage at the market place. Their take-home pay figures out to be 35 cents a day greater than a fellow worker from Brunswick drawing the same wage. And in addition to the cost of tolls, the migrant worker has gasoline costs and automobile wear and tear to consider. This latter cost can be significant when you consider the fact all coastal Georgia cars engines are calibrated to run on level ground, and negotiating those two arched causeway bridges places a tremendous strain on the motors.

All of us can help by pitching in and doing our share. Just think of those few extra pennies you pay for a bottle of milk as a donation to help the poor St. Simons dairy farmer stay in business, and feel glad you are able to pay a paltry buck or two extra for a pair of socks to keep a struggling Sea Island shop keeper from going under. Remember when you go to restaurants to ask the servers where they are from before you leave a tip, and always keep in mind the slogan: Buy St. Simons -- sometimes shortened to BSS, or even further to plain BS.

38. BEARS

Yankees are not particularly fond of wild bears, and several have asked if there were any in Georgia. I personally have never seen one and can confidently state there are none on St. Simons or Jekyll Island, at least not in the built-up areas; but for an authoritative answer concerning the rest of Georgia, I consulted Scar Face Fenston, who is probably the foremost authority on Georgia bears in the whole world. In fact, rumor has it that Scar Face was brought up by a kindly mother bear when he was abandoned at a rural drive-in theater shortly after birth. I do not know if this rumor is true, but no one who has ever met Scar Face is inclined to discard it completely.

First of all, Scar Face assures me Georgia bears do not eat Yankees, as some Southerners would have you believe. As a matter of fact, he tells me most of them have never even tasted a Yankee. To further allay Yankee apprehension, he claims Georgia black bears are quite benign, compared to their western brown bear cousins, and will generally run the other way when they see a human.

This comforting information should be tempered with the realization that the word "benign" is here used in a comparative sense. You should also take note of the word "generally."

Scar Face further discourages complacency by mentioning there is an exception to the "run-the-other-way" rule. It is the mother bear with cubs. Apparently the papa bear cannot care less what happens to his offspring, but the mama bear can be very nasty if anyone gets between her and her cubs. Therefore, the first thing to do when you come upon a bear in the Georgia wilds is to determine if it is a mama bear or a papa bear.

In actual practice it is probably best to assume any bear you come upon is a mama bear, because wild bear sex identification can be a tricky thing. This is particularly so if the bear happens to be running, and most particularly if it happens to be running toward the identifier.

Having determined, or assumed, the bear is a mother, the next step is to locate her offspring. There will usually be two of them and they will be running like mad to get to the side of you opposite their mother. Do not let them do so. When they sense danger, mama bears tend to run in a straight line for those cubs, not unlike a freight train. You do not want to be in that line of run.

A good way to get out of the way is to climb a tree. Of course, bears can also climb trees, but Scar Face claims most mama bears are only interested in getting to their young and leading them away. So once you are up a tree, you have nothing to worry about, unless, of course, there happens to be a bear cub in the upper branches of the tree. It is important to select a bear-free tree as refuge.

And do not worry about being able to get up that tree. All Yankees carry a deeply-embedded prehistoric tree-climbing instinct which is triggered by the sight of a wild bear.

39. GRITS

Most Yankees do not realize the special place grits occupy in the Southern psyche. Grits are to the South as cheese is to France, potatoes to Ireland, maple syrup to Vermont. It is not just a question of taste. It is a question of culture and heritage. Sir Walter Raleigh broke the ice with Pocahontas over a bowl of grits. General Lee and Jackson planned the Battle of Chancellorsville during a late supper of grits. Grits are the South.

All this comes as a surprise to the newly-arrived Yankee, because he has never before tasted grits. Grits simply do not exist only a few miles north of the Mason Dixon Line. This is because grits cannot be successfully manufactured or prepared up north. It has something to do with the co-inductation of confluent flux waves emanating from residual traces of the aurora borealis.

Eskimos live out their lives without ever experiencing the rapture of eating grits, and many Northerners do too. But among the more enlightened Yankees who have ventured south are a growing number of genuine grit fanciers, although Yankee palates will never catch up to Southern taste buds when it comes to grit appreciation.

For example, Yankees tend to eat grits only at breakfast, and they put milk and sugar on them rather than butter. Being a tolerant people, Southerners go along with this Yankee idiosyncrasy, and most Southern restaurants offer grits on the breakfast menu, served by waitresses who are trained to keep a straight face.

Unlike their Yankee cousins, Southerners eat grits with all meals, and they prepare them in an infinite number of ways: boiled, baked, fried, steamed, sauteed, braised, blanched, and barbecued. And because grits so readily blend with other foods, there are a large variety of tantalizing grit dishes, many of them reflecting regional gastronomic preferences. Thus, there are Cajun blackened grits, Georgia peach grits, Kentucky bourbon grits, Mississippi possum grits, and so on. Unfortunately, Yankees seldom get a chance to sample these great grit dishes because Southerners try very hard to limit foreign intake of grits. They realize that the eating of grits is what causes and nurtures the Southern drawl, and they do not want any Yankee impostors infiltrating their ranks.

However, Yankees may some day be consuming volumes of grits in another form. As the fear of tobacco-induced cancer swept the land, an ingenious rural Georgia inventor set about finding a grits-based tobacco substitute. As any grit expert well knows, grits are not only free from cancer-causing substances, they are mostly fat free and contain almost no cholesterol at all.

The inventor, one Phinecrious W. Rawly -- a distant relative of Sir Walter, who was a notoriously bad speller -- has made great strides in his quest. Because the Association of United Tobacco Growers has put a contract out on him, Phinecrious works in a secret laboratory tucked away in the pine thickets of south-central Georgia and emerges only infrequently, and in deep disguise, to announce his progress. He has experienced some trouble keeping grits lit when packed in pipes or cigarettes -- particularly if butter is added to them -- but he is almost ready to market some smokeless products. For the health-concerned tobacco chewer, he has developed a chewing grits which will eventually be sold under the trade name, Green Man -- named in honor of a former colleague who was employed as a product tester during the early stages of development. It is a blend of grits, mouthwash, and bubble gum. The mouthwash enhances social acceptability. The bubble gum provides elasticity and discourages swallowing.

Difficulty was also experienced in developing a substitute for snuff. Grit kernels kept lodging athwart sinuses and clogging nasal passages, but Phinecrious ingeniously solved the problem by coating the grit kernels with a slippery substance made from a secret formula and manufactured in Columbia. Those who have tested the product claim it is far more satisfying than the tobacco-based snuff it was designed to replace. The "grit sniff," as it is called, will be sold in delicately carved and highly polished sniff boxes, suitable for use by both ladies and gentlemen. That will surely be collectors items someday.

Although neither Green Man nor grit sniff has actually made it to the marketplace as of this writing, both are being packaged as you read this by a small hand-picked work force of intensely loyal workers. Indeed those involved in the carving, polishing, and packing of the sniff boxes are so excited about the product, they are working a twelve-hour day at half pay. With workers like that, how can Phinecrious Enterprises possibly fail?

And the best news of all, as far as Yankees are concerned, is that the bubble gum and Columbian slippery coating seem to protect the grits from the debilitating influence of the aurora borealis. Not only will the products be sold in the South, they will also be available to Yankees -- and even Eskimos. Watch for them on the shelves of your favorite market.

40. THE GREAT BLIZZARD OF '89

Yankees who have come to the Golden Isles in recent years are not likely to have heard of the area's snow fall. It is not something that gets a lot of local publicity. To most Northerners the idea of snow standing on the beaches of Coastal Georgia is as far fetched as George Burns developing a bad case of acne. But that is exactly what occurred in December of 1989.

The freak snowfall was preceded by several hours of freezing rain that coated everything with ice, thereby assuring a nice cold surface to preserve the snow and close down the causeway linking St. Simons to the rest of Georgia.

Not much damage was suffered, no lives were lost, and the snow melted soon after the sun came out, but as far as traumatic experience was concerned, the blizzard ranked right up there with the Chicago Fire and the Johnstown Flood.

Electricity stopped flowing, water pipes froze, the Coast Guard started patrolling for icebergs, the wind howled, and many Southerners took to their beds to shiver beneath several layers of blankets. It is said that many of them did not venture out from under those covers until mid-April, but these reports were obviously exaggerated. Most of my southern friends were up and about by the first of February.

The storm was also hard on animals. Great herds of alligators migrated southward through the driving snow, and little Southern female dogs were devastated. I know a lady whose miniature poodle, Scarlett, came in after that first squat in the snow and refused thereafter ever to leave the house again.

The only ones who welcomed the chaos were the soldiers of the St. Simons Republican Army, the underground militant arm of the Burn The Bridge Movement, which advocates St. Simons independence from Glynn County. Since most of its members are Yankees, a sizable number of the SSRA were able to assemble at a local watering hole to plot the overthrow of the crippled government. Armed with snow balls reinforced with chunks of gravel, patrols fanned out to ambush Glynn County police cruisers, while members of the military council quaffed root beer and issued orders throughout the night. Nothing much came of the uprising. Task forces sent out to take over the reins of government were not able to find anyone holding the reins -- nor any reins, for that matter. The combat patrols found not a single police cruiser, although a detachment ran across an empty Glynn County highway repair crew porta-potty which was quickly captured in the name of the Republic. Eventually the sun came up, the root beer ran out, the flag of revolution was hauled down from the porta-potty, and the Republican Army melted back into the shadows to await the next opportunity to do in the County of Glynn.

As often happens the crisis brought out both the best and worst in human nature. A Yankee resident was seen giving free lessons in how to walk on snow-covered ice without falling down, but there were some who sought personal gain from the disaster. I was visiting up North at the time and first heard of the storm when I received a call from a local friend who blurted, "You wouldn't believe what snow shovels are selling for down in the village. Load up your car with about four dozen and get back down here." Needless to say, I immediately delivered to my friend a lecture on the evils of exploitation. But

Yankee ingenuity had a whole host of needed supplies on their way by nightfall from as far away as Nome, Alaska.

The day after the storm the snow began to melt and a short time thereafter the warm Georgia sunshine had Yankee enterprise in full retreat. The cases of emergency canned goods which began to pile up were eventually sold at cost to those who worried about hurricanes, but snow plows and dog sleds were a total loss. One Yankee got rid of a dozen Saint Bernard dogs only by offering them for sale, at discount, as Yankee possum hounds. Southern hunters didn't think much of their hunting ability, but they liked the little casks of brandy hooked to their collars.

Once the snow had vanished and the Coast Guard had given the all clear to coastal shipping, local weather forecasters came out of hiding to theorize on the cause of the hundred year event. There were several explanations offered, but the most logical one placed the blame on the "El Yankino," a current of super cold water which appears mysteriously to surge down the inland waterway and play hob with the upper atmospheric Southern weather patterns. Very little is known about the dreaded "El Yankino," except that it is of short duration, originates deep in Yankee waters, and is totally unpredictable.

I realize all this is somewhat "old hat" to the old timers living along the Georgia Coast, but I am writing not for them, but for you newcomers to the Golden Isles. It is important you realize the area is not completely disaster-proof, as you may have thought. It is true that blizzards are rare in these parts, but when it comes to that "El Yankino," you can never be sure. Thus, it might be prudent to lay in a few tins of corned beef, just to be on the safe side, and there are those who claim that while it may never be used, a snowmobile stashed away in a St. Simons basement pays for itself in terms of peace of mind.

And, incidentally, if any of you would like to buy a snow shovel, I have a few which I will sell cheap.

41. NO-SEE-UMS

Seldom mentioned in tourist brochures are the swarms of voracious little gnats the Yankee encounters soon after arriving in the Golden Isles. They are known colloquially as "no-see-ums," for they are so tiny they are very nearly invisible. What there is of them seems to be made up mostly of jaws. They are also known locally by several other names, but most of them are unprintable.

These nasty little biters inhabit the Marshes of Glynn in great number and feed exclusively on Yankees. I did not believe it when I was first told this, but after watching Yankees frantically swatting their arms and necks while nearby Southerners lounged about looking blasé, I became a believer. But then, quite by accident, I stumbled upon the truth: insect repellent.

Yankees instinctively shy away from using insect repellent against anything they cannot see. The whole idea smacks of witchcraft. But I can assure you, insect repellents work. There are several suitable products available, but I am not in the business of endorsing products, so you will just have to find them yourself. However, there are a couple of home remedies which I am happy to pass on, although I have not tried them myself.

One is simply home-made Georgia corn liquor, also known as white lightning, hooch, etc. It is not known whether the insects are repelled by the smell or die from getting fumes in their nostrils, but it works fairly well. It also has a side advantage. If you take a few swallows, you no longer care whether you are being bitten by insects or not. But if you do this, you should avoid being around an open flame.

The second repellent is called Ocean Delight. Its main ingredient is fermenting fish, blended with garlic and onions. It is both powerful and cheap. A whole gallon goes for about thirty eight cents on the local market, although if Vidalia onions are used it may cost ten or fifteen cents more. Yankees can expect to pay up to three bucks for it.

However, from what I hear, ~~Sea Breeze~~ is well worth the money. It not only fends off the "no-see-ums," it also repels mosquitoes, ticks, alligators, cats, dogs, and humans. Many Southerners swear by it, although Southern wives generally are not among its fans.

The final remedy I address is sold commercially as a skin conditioner for women with dry skin. It smells like a very large pansy with over-developed scent glands. For some reason, it works well against "noseeums," particularly for women. It also works for men, but there are drawbacks. Indoors it gives off a super strong odor.

If you happen to be a man and have it on when you come indoors, be prepared to hear women titter and have other men look at you sort of funny. And, whatever you do, stay away from bars.

There are bars here in Georgia where it is far better to smell like a fermenting fish than a giant pansy.

42. FREDERICA ENHANCEMENT

A friend of mine from out West became all upset when he had to pay two dollars to visit Frederica National Monument here on St. Simons. He claimed that during a recent visit to Yellowstone National Park, he only shelled out two bucks to see towering geysers, lots of bears, and a bunch of bull elk trumpeting a loud echoing cry to attract females and warn off competing males. In fact, according to my friend and a special report on national television, people come from all over the world during the mating season to line the breeding grounds of the Yellowstone elk, just to hear that trumpeting. And not a one of them pays over two dollars for the electrifying experience.

Of course, I immediately jumped to the defense of Fort Frederica and asked my friend if his great Yellowstone had towering live oaks and the ruins of an old historic fort and a vine that was 150 years old and a ranger who could wiggle his ears. That stopped him of course, but I have to admit my friend may have a point. It would appear that either the entrance fee to Frederica should be lowered, or the Yellowstone admission raised, or the Frederica attractions enhanced. After giving the matter some thought, I think the last course is the best. Utilizing available resources and a modest investment of capital, a truly memorable display could be developed.

To answer the trumpeting of the bull elk, Frederica could establish a colony of alligators along the banks of the Frederica River and feature the trumpeting of the bull alligator. Many people do not realize bull alligators trumpet during the mating season, but they do, and the sound is most impressive, particularly to female alligators. The problem is the trumpeting is so softly done, one has to get his ear right down close to the bull alligator's mouth in order to hear it.

Few have ever experienced the sound, since most people do not like to get their ears—or anything else, for that matter—down close to an alligator's mouth. Doubtless Frederica visitors share this aversion, but the difficulty can be overcome through electronic enhancement. By strategically placing microphones among the alligators and beaming the sound through loudspeakers concealed along the river bank, we should be able to expand the volume enough to not only accommodate hard of hearing spectators, but to lure lady alligators all the way from Sapelo Island.

Or, better still, we can record the trumpeting and play back the tapes. This will allow us to keep the mating season going all year long for the convenience of visitors. Just imagine the thrill of sitting on the ramparts of Fort Frederica on a warm summer afternoon listening to plaintive cries of lovesick alligators while sipping Gatorade sold by the Fort Frederica Association. The Association could make additional money by selling little alligator mementos and a children's book entitled: Phoebe and the Amorous Alligators.

As for bears, it would cost little to capture three nice Georgia black bears in the Okefenokee Swamp. Securely tethered, they could be led about the Frederica ruins by the park Rangers to delight young and old alike. Everyone likes bears, particularly if they are tethered. We could also teach the bears to wear ranger hats, thereby disseminating a subtle reminder to prevent forest fires.

There is no reason why we could not add exhibitions of bear wrestling to further flesh out the program. Contrary to popular belief, bear wrestling is not all that difficult or dangerous. The bears are tightly muzzled to prevent biting and any average robust person can easily master the art. All he, or she, needs is a grasp of the basic principles of leverage and enough agility to avoid being fallen upon by the bear. I am fully confident any of the fine Rangers currently assigned to Fort Frederica can easily become accomplished bear wrestlers.

Geysers would be difficult to duplicate, although minor adjustments to the water fountain just outside the visitors center would make it, if not exactly an Old Faithful, at least an interesting visitor challenge and spectator favorite. However, geyser creation would not be necessary. Those wrestling bears and trumpeting bull alligators, together with the existing ruins, live oaks, and old vines, should rocket Fort Frederica right up there with Disney World as a major East Coast tourist attraction. And for two bucks, not even Yellowstone could come close in the value category.

As a matter of fact, I would gladly pay two dollars just to see one of the Frederica Rangers wrestle a bear.

43. TREES

A St. Simons motorist driving south on Demere is suddenly confronted by a warning sign that says,"CAUTION, TREES NEAR ROADWAY." If the motorist happens to be a newly-arrived Yankee, he is likely to be confused. A Yankee is familiar with signs that warn of "children playing near road" or "cows" or "deer" or various other things which could suddenly dart out in front of a car. However, as far as he is concerned, trees do not dart out in front of cars, at least not up North they don't.

Then the Yankee reconsiders and arrives at a logical conclusion. He assumes the warning is to protect his car from damage it might suffer if he drives too close to one of those trees. And he is wrong again.

That sign is not there to protect passing cars any more than a "CHILDREN PLAYING" sign is placed to prevent the denting of fenders by careless children. That sign is there to protect the trees. Glenn County officials are very touchy when it comes to trees.

All this was demonstrated recently by Mrs. Katrina Vanderhooter, a proud Yankee lady of impressive lineage who lives in my neighborhood. Mrs. Vanderhooter, who has had trouble with trees before, swears one of the Demere Oaks really did jump out in front of her car one morning. Swerving to avoid it, she collided with one of its companions standing close to the edge of the road.

She explained all this to the investigating officer, but he was not very sympathetic. He not only issued her a ticket for reckless driving, he required her to take a breathometer test right on the spot.

It was all very traumatic and most embarrassing to Katrina, who had once been the president of the WCTU in her Connecticut home town and who refuses to have so much as a bottle of rubbing alcohol in her home. To make matters worse, the screaming sirens of the arriving ambulance and fire engines attracted a large crowd of onlookers to witness her humiliation.

Fortunately, Katrina was not hurt physically. And this was just as well, since she was completely ignored by the ambulance rescue squad and the accompanying doctor, who turned out to be a tree surgeon. Few people realize that tree surgeons on St. Simons are on call to join ambulance crews responding to accidents involving trees.

This particular surgeon was very good, according to Mrs. Vanderhooter. He had the tree stabilized, treated for shock, and its wound bandaged before she had completed the breathometer test.

Although Katrina may not share my sentiments, I for one appreciate the concern shown our trees by the authorities of Glynn County and call for a large round of applause for these sensitive public servants. I hope all you Yankees out there will join me in awarding them a hearty Huzza! and remember them in your prayers.

I also hope you will exercise care when driving past those trees on the edge of Demere Road. In all probability Mrs. Vanderhooter only imagined one of them jumped in front of her. But here in the Golden Isles, we cannot be all that sure.

44. FINALLY

In conclusion, I pass on the answers to some to the more frequently asked questions by both Yankee and Southerners.

QUES: "After observing Yankee driving habits, I am wondering if Yankee states require driver exams before issuing licenses."

ANS: Yes, they do; but driving rules vary from one state to another. For example, some Northern states waive the requirement to use turn signals for anyone short enough to look through the steering wheel when they drive. However, these people are required to drive at half the posted speed limit.

QUES: "Can you tell me why on earth Georgia men leave on their baseball hats when eating at a public restaurant?"

ANS: Yes I can. You have Mrs. W. P. O'Mally, housewife and mother from Calhoun County to thank for this. Her four teenage sons kept losing or misplacing their hats, and she grew tired of buying new ones for them. She developed, and eventually patented, an adhesive which securely holds hats in place. It is composed of chewing gum, crazy glue, peanut butter, and mucilage. Unfortunately, it takes several years for the concoction to soften enough for the hats to be taken off, and during that time, hats remain firmly affixed to the heads -- indoors, outdoors, and in restaurants. Eventually the idea was embraced by mothers and wives throughout the country. It became a fad, and now the majority of young American males wear their hats everywhere.

QUES: "Where do the wild horses on Cumberland Island come from? Did the old Spanish have anything to do with it?"

ANS: The wild horses come from wild mares. They start out as wild foals, become wild colts, and eventually grow into wild horses. The old Spanish had nothing to do with it.

QUES: "Why do young men wear earrings?"

ANS: Most of those earrings you see dangling from young male ears are really miniature hearing aids. You see, the music embraced by the youth of today is so loud, most of them suffer from a severe loss of hearing. This is particularly true of rock musicians. By disguising their hearing aids as earrings, they avoid the stigma of appearing to be members of the mature generation, who stick their hearing aids in their ears.

QUES: "Since being down South, I have heard the yellow lines running up the center of roads referred to as Yankee bicycle lanes. Is that what they are?"

ANS: No -- except in Atlanta.

QUES: "I heard that for short distances alligators can sprint faster than a man can run. Is that true? And if it is, do you have any suggestions on how to get away from a pursuing alligator?"

ANS: Unfortunately it is true. Fortunately there is a method of eluding a pursuing alligator. It comes from a wise lady who lives on Sapelo Island. She advises to run in tight zigzags. Alligators are top heavy and tend to tip over when making tight turns. This gives you an opportunity to make good your escape or, if you prefer, to run back and tickle the under belly of the upside down beast. If possible, use a feather to do this. Alligators are easily tranquilized by tickling their stomachs with a feather. They will remain in a state of alligator bliss until someone from the Georgia Department of Wild Life arrives to take them to Sea Island -- or wherever errant alligators are taken.

QUES: "I know you have assured us alligators don't eat Yankees. But are you really sure?"

ANS: Well,....................pretty sure.